# Provincial Cooking of Canada

*Culinary Arts Institute*

# Foreword

Modern Canadian cuisine is the product of years of development and adaptation of cooking methods brought from the European homes of the settlers who now make up our nation. In this strange new country they found foods they had never seen before, and they also found Canada's native Indians eating foods and using techniques completely new to them. From them they learned to eat buffalo, pincherries, saskatoons, wild rice, and various kinds of tea.

With two of the world's greatest oceans at Canada's shores, it is little wonder that the Atlantic and Pacific fisheries yield up seafood in great quantity and variety, and, due to the cold northern water, of excellent quality. The Atlantic provinces are, therefore, famous for fish and the recipes adapted by the French, Scots, and Irish who settled there. Newfoundland, where there is little soil for raising meat or vegetables, has made use of fish in an original and fascinating way: in the section devoted to that province will be found recipes for baked cods' tongues and flipper pie.

Quebec is a treasure chest of recipes based on French cookery and adapted to Canadian produce. Many French-Canadian recipes 300 years old are still in use, and Quebec pea soup, onion soup, and tourtière (a special pork pie) are known all over Canada and far beyond.

Ontario, like Quebec, produces that glorious maple syrup and maple sugar that can be used in so many ways. It also produces many freshwater fish; in fact, freshwater fish may be said to be one of Canada's specialities, since Canada has one third of all the fresh water in the world. Ontario also has magnificent orchards and market gardens, and it produces 90 per cent of all the wine made in Canada. Many of these wines now compare favorably with imported wines and add a pleasant complement to Canadian meals. In its section is a recipe for making honey without bees; the recipe dates from the 17th century and it really works!

The Prairie Provinces—sometimes called the breadbasket of the world—produce many grains, among them the famous hard wheat developed in Canada's Experimental Farm. Western beef is generally regarded as the best in the world, because the calves are milk-fed longer than most. A whole young steer barbecued in a pit produces some of the most succulent eating obtainable anywhere.

British Columbia excels in fish, vegetables, and fruits. Two of the latter that are rarely found outside the province are loganberries, a cross between raspberries and blackberries developed on Vancouver Island, and giant Zucca melons.

Each section of recipes deals with a particular province, and the recipes have been selected to give a cross-section of the foods native to that province and to suggest ways of preparing them that are either traditional in the area or that bring out the best in flavor. A choice of recipes, starting with appetizers or soup and including fish, meat, vegetables, and desserts, will enable readers to make up their own menus for a delicious Canadian meal.

Many visitors to Canada enjoy fishing and hunting, and recipes have been included for fish or game that they may catch. Of course some foods are only available fresh during certain seasons, and some, alas, are not available outside the province where they grow. But we can always do as our ancestors did, and improvise and substitute. Sweetgrass Buffalo and Beer Pie is very good made with beef, and other fish besides Arctic char respond well to marinades and barbecuing.

Good Luck and *Bon Appétit!*

Copyright © 1975, 1983 by
Delair Publishing Company, Inc.
420 Lexington Avenue,
New York, New York 10170

ISBN: 0-8326-0579-4

# BRITISH COLUMBIA

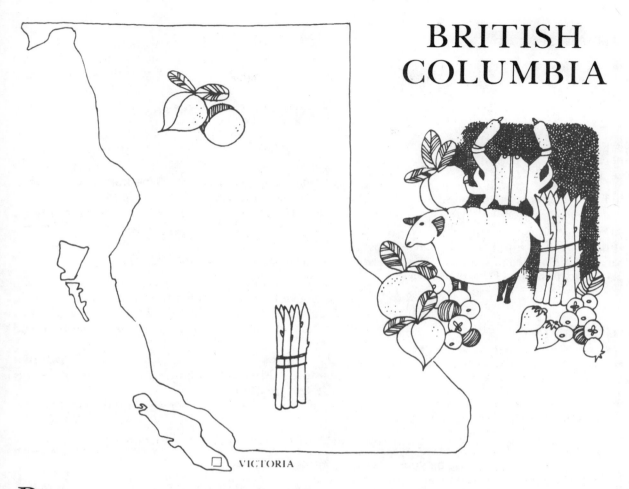

VICTORIA

B ritish Columbia is noted for the variety and quality of its fish and for the riches of its market gardens and orchards. Add to these the tradition of all that is best in English cooking, and dining out in British Columbia can be a very special experience.

British Columbia salmon fight their way up the Fraser River in the spring to spawning grounds, helped where necessary by man-made fish-ladders. (These may be seen at Hope and Spuzzum.) There are five varieties of salmon — sockeye, spring, coho, chum, and pink — and huge quantities are canned every year. The Pacific coast also yields up halibut, some of which reach between 400 and 500 pounds each, black cod, and shellfish, which include shrimp, oysters, and the large, delicious King crab.

In addition to the wealth of fruit that may be eaten raw, there are red and black currants and gooseberries to be made into jams and jellies.

Then there are delectable wines, made with the native fruits — loganberry wine, blackberry cordial, strawberry wine, and so on.

A special treat are Victoria Creams, chocolate bonbons made since 1885 from a still-secret recipe, which are exported all over the world.

## OYSTER COCKTAIL

| | |
|---|---|
| 10 oysters | ¼ teaspoon Tabasco |
| 2 tablespoons ketchup | 1 teaspoon lemon juice |
| 1 tablespoon grated horseradish | Few grains salt |
| | 2 lemon slices |
| ¼ teaspoon Worcestershire sauce | |

1. Shuck oysters and rinse with cold water to remove any grit.
2. Blend remaining ingredients to make a sauce.
3. Put five oysters into each tall glass and spoon sauce over them. Garnish each with a lemon slice. Chill and serve.

2 SERVINGS

## NUTTY SHRIMP SPREAD

¾ cup chopped cooked shrimp

¼ cup chopped ripe olives

¼ cup chopped walnuts

3 to 4 tablespoons mayonnaise-type salad dressing

1 tablespoon lemon juice

¼ teaspoon thyme

¼ teaspoon salt

Few grains cayenne pepper

1. Combine all ingredients and blend well. Refrigerate until thoroughly chilled.

2. To serve, spread on crisp *crackers*, and if desired, sprinkle with additional chopped walnuts. Garnish each with a *piece of shrimp*, a whole *small shrimp*, or a sprig of *parsley*.

ABOUT 1⅓ CUPS SPREAD

## SHRIMP BOAT TARTLETS

*Imaginative and wondrously successful is this blending of tart cranberries with the delicate flavor of shrimp.*

1 cup fresh cranberries

½ cup apricot nectar

¼ cup sugar

½ teaspoon grated lemon peel

Pie crust mix for a 2-crust pie

Garlic powder

1 cup finely chopped celery

Fresh small shrimp, cooked, peeled, deveined, and chilled in French dressing marinade

1. Combine the cranberries, apricot nectar, sugar, and lemon peel in a saucepan. Bring to boiling and cook, stirring occasionally, until cranberries are tender, about 2 minutes. Cool, then chill.

2. Prepare pie crust mix according to package directions. Divide dough in half and shape into two balls.

3. Cut two 12-inch squares of aluminum foil. Roll out each half of pastry on a foil square, covering the square evenly. Cut pie crust and foil together into twenty-four 4x3-inch pieces. Sprinkle the pastry lightly with garlic powder.

4. Brush the 3-inch edges of pastry with water. Fold the foil-covered pastry rectangles lengthwise. Pinch the ends together and shape into "boats" with flat bottoms. Place on a baking sheet.

5. Bake at 425°F 10 to 12 minutes, or until lightly browned. Cool and remove foil.

6. Spoon some celery into each boat; top with drained shrimp and then with the whole cooked cranberries and sauce. Serve at once.

2 DOZEN APPETIZERS

## ZESTY SHRIMP TEMPTERS

2 cups cider vinegar

½ cup water

¼ cup salt

¼ teaspoon black pepper

2 tablespoons sugar

3 bay leaves

½ teaspoon whole allspice

½ teaspoon whole cloves

½ teaspoon whole mustard seed

⅛ teaspoon paprika

3 medium-sized onions, sliced

4 lbs. large fresh shrimp, cooked, peeled, and deveined

1. Combine the vinegar and water in a saucepan. Bring to boiling. Remove from heat and stir in salt, pepper, and sugar until dissolved. Stir in the bay leaves, allspice, cloves, mustard seed, paprika, and onion.

2. Put cooked shrimp into a large bowl (not metal). Add vinegar mixture and mix gently. Cover; refrigerate 24 hours.

3. Before serving, drain shrimp thoroughly. Arrange on a bed of frilly *green lettuce leaves*. Accompany with fancy cocktail picks.

ABOUT 4 DOZEN SHRIMP

## CRAB-FLAKE ROLL-UPS

10 thin slices very soft bread

¼ cup butter or margarine, melted

½ teaspoon grated lemon peel

1 teaspoon lemon juice

1 cup drained canned crab meat

2 tablespoons mayonnaise

2 teaspoons finely chopped parsley

½ teaspoon prepared mustard

½ teaspoon prepared horseradish

¼ teaspoon salt

1. Trim crusts from bread; roll each slice lightly with a rolling pin.

2. Combine butter with lemon peel and lemon juice. Brush bread slices lightly with about half of the lemon butter.

3. Remove any bony tissue from crab; separate into fine flakes. Mix thoroughly with remaining ingredients.

4. Spread bread slices with crab mixture; roll slices up jelly-roll fashion; secure with wooden picks. Brush tops with remaining lemon butter.

5. Place roll-ups on a baking sheet. Toast under broiler heat about 5 minutes, turning to brown lightly on all sides.                    10 ROLL-UPS

## DUTCH CHRISTMAS LOAVES

| | |
|---|---|
| 1 cup milk, scalded | 4 eggs, well beaten |
| 1 cup butter or margarine, melted | 1 tablespoon grated lemon peel |
| 1 cup sugar | 1 cup (about 7 oz.) chopped citron |
| 1 teaspoon salt | |
| 2 pkgs. active dry yeast | 1 cup raisins, plumped |
| ½ cup warm water | 1½ cups finely chopped blanched almonds |
| 7 cups all-purpose flour | |

1. Pour milk over butter, sugar, and salt in bowl; cool to lukewarm.
2. Soften yeast in the warm water.
3. Add about 1 cup of the flour to the milk mixture and beat vigorously until smooth. Stir in the yeast. Add half the remaining flour; beat well.
4. Beat in the eggs and lemon peel with the remaining flour to make a smooth dough. Stir in the fruits and nuts until distributed evenly. Cover; let rise in a warm place until doubled, about 1½ hours.
5. Divide dough into halves; shape each into a ball and place in two greased and floured 9-inch layer cake pans. Cover; let rise again until doubled, 1 to 1½ hours.
6. Bake at 375°F about 40 minutes, or until browned. Remove from pans and cool on racks. Brush with *melted butter* and sprinkle with *confectioners' (icing) sugar*.      2 LOAVES BREAD

## SHRIMP STUFFED EGGS IN TOMATO SAUCE

| | |
|---|---|
| 12 hard-cooked eggs | ¼ cup finely chopped onion |
| ⅓ cup salad dressing or mayonnaise | 1 tablespoon snipped parsley |
| 1 teaspoon Worcestershire sauce | |
| 6 drops Tabasco | Cooked shelled shrimp |
| 1 teaspoon dry mustard | Tomato Sauce, *below* |

1. Cut the eggs lengthwise into halves. Remove yolks, keeping whites intact. Sieve the egg yolks; mix in salad dressing, Worcestershire sauce, Tabasco, dry mustard, onion, and parsley.
2. Fill egg whites with the yolk mixture, rounding tops. Arrange a shrimp, rounded side up, on each egg half, pressing slightly.
3. Place stuffed eggs in a buttered shallow 2-quart rectangular baking dish. Spoon sauce around eggs so that shrimp and stuffing show.
4. Set in a 325°F oven 10 to 15 minutes, or until eggs are heated. Garnish with *parsley sprigs*.
                           ABOUT 12 SERVINGS
**TOMATO SAUCE:** Heat *2 tablespoons cooking or salad oil* in a heavy saucepan. Add *½ cup finely chopped onion* and *½ cup finely chopped green pepper;* cook until tender, stirring occasionally. Stir in *2 pimientos*, chopped, and *2 cups canned tomato sauce;* simmer about 10 minutes to blend flavors.                    2⅓ CUPS SAUCE

## BRAN GEMS

| | |
|---|---|
| 1 cup sifted all-purpose flour | 1 cup whole bran cereal |
| ⅓ cup sugar | 1 egg, well beaten |
| 1 tablespoon baking powder | ⅔ cup milk |
| ½ teaspoon salt | 3 tablespoons butter or margarine, melted |

1. Sift flour, sugar, baking powder, and salt together into a bowl; stir in bran cereal.
2. Combine egg, milk, and melted butter. Add to flour mixture and stir quickly and lightly only enough to moisten. Spoon batter equally into greased 1¾x1-inch muffin-pan wells.
3. Bake at 400°F 25 to 30 minutes. Immediately loosen and tip muffins in wells. Serve warm.
                           ABOUT 10 MUFFINS

## WHOLE WHEAT PEAR BREAD

| | |
|---|---|
| 2 to 3 fresh Bartlett pears | 1 egg, beaten |
| 2 tablespoons shortening | 1 cup sifted all-purpose flour |
| 1 teaspoon grated lemon peel | 1 teaspoon baking soda |
| ⅔ cup firmly packed light brown sugar | 1 teaspoon salt |
| ½ cup honey | ½ teaspoon ground cinnamon |
| 2 tablespoons lemon juice | ¼ teaspoon ground cloves |
| ⅓ cup water | 1 cup whole wheat flour |
| | 1 cup chopped walnuts |

1. Core pears, but do not peel. Cut lengthwise slices from one pear and reserve to decorate top of

bread. Dice enough remaining pears to measure 1 cup.

2. Mix shortening, grated lemon peel, and brown sugar in a bowl. Add honey, lemon juice, water, and egg; mix well.

3. Sift all-purpose flour, baking soda, salt, cinnamon, and cloves; stir in whole wheat flour. Add flour mixture to liquid mixture, stirring just enough to moisten flour. Mix in walnuts and diced pears. Turn into a greased 9x5x3-inch loaf pan and arrange reserved pear slices crosswise along center.

4. Bake at 325°F 70 to 75 minutes.

5. Cool bread 10 minutes in pan on wire rack; remove from pan and cool completely before slicing or storing.        1 LOAF BREAD

## SALTSPRING LAMB

Tender little lambs, raised on the salty marshes of Saltspring Island, roasted and served with fresh mint sauce, have an exquisite flavor all their own.

Ashcroft Potatoes—British Columbia's answer to Idaho potatoes—could be baked while the lamb is roasting and, of course, tiny new peas from British Columbia's famous market gardens are the perfect accompaniment.

## OYSTER-APPLE STUFFING

| | |
|---|---|
| 1 cup butter | 2 cups water |
| ⅔ cup finely chopped turkey giblets | 24 slices dry bread, cut in cubes |
| 1 pt. oysters | 2½ teaspoons salt |
| 2½ cups finely chopped celery | ¼ teaspoon black pepper |
| 1 cup finely chopped onion | 1 teaspoon sage |
| | ½ teaspoon sugar |
| 1½ cups grated apple (about 4 medium, pared) | 2 eggs, beaten |

1. Heat ½ cup of the butter in a heavy skillet. Add giblets and cook over medium heat 20 minutes, stirring occasionally.

2. Drain the oysters; remove any shell particles. Coarsely chop and refrigerate until ready to use.

3. Heat remaining ½ cup butter in a large skillet. Add celery, onion, and apple; cook over medium heat until onion is soft, stirring occasionally.

4. Meanwhile, pour water over bread cubes.

Sprinkle with a mixture of salt, pepper, sage, and sugar; toss gently. Add eggs and mix lightly. Blend in oysters, giblets, and apple mixture. Lightly spoon into body and neck cavities of bird (do not pack).

STUFFING FOR A 15-POUND TURKEY

## PRINCE RUPERT BLACK COD

*This fish was soaked in brine before it was delicately smoked over pine boughs.*

| | |
|---|---|
| 2 lbs. smoked black cod | ½ cup milk |
| Cold water | Lemon Butter Sauce, *below* |

1. Put cod into a skillet or saucepan. Cover fish with cold water. Cover skillet. Bring water to simmering over low heat and simmer 1 minute. Drain. Repeat process once or twice depending on saltiness of fish. Simmer in last water until fish is cooked. Allow about 10 minutes cooking time per inch thickness of fish.

2. Put cooked cod into a greased baking dish and pour milk over cod.

3. Bake at 350°F 10 minutes, or until milk is hot.

4. Serve fish with Lemon Butter Sauce. Garnish with *parsley*.        ABOUT 6 SERVINGS

## LEMON BUTTER SAUCE

| | |
|---|---|
| 2 tablespoons lemon juice (or lime juice for variety) | ¼ cup melted butter Salt and pepper to taste |

Mix ingredients.        ABOUT ⅓ CUP SAUCE

## MARINATED SALMON

| | |
|---|---|
| 2 lbs. salmon steaks* | ½ cup lemon juice |
| 3 onions, sliced | 1 small piece ginger root |
| 1½ teaspoons salt | 2 blades mace |
| 3 cups boiling water | 4 coriander seeds |
| 1 cup dry white wine | 1 bay leaf |
| ½ cup white wine vinegar | 6 peppercorns |

1. Place fish in a wire basket or on a plate. If using a plate, tie it in a piece of cheesecloth. Put onion into a deep skillet or saucepan; sprinkle with salt and pour in boiling water. Bring to boiling; put fish into water. Reduce heat and simmer about 10 minutes, or until fish is opaque and flakes easily. Carefully remove fish and drain. Arrange on a platter or in a shallow bowl. Set aside to cool.

2. Strain stock. Combine 2 cups of the stock and

remaining ingredients in a saucepan. Bring to boiling; boil 5 minutes. Pour over fish. Chill at least 24 hours before serving.

3.  Serve cold garnished with *sliced hard-cooked egg*, if desired.  6 TO 8 SERVINGS

*Pickerel, pike, or whitefish may be used instead of salmon.

## PLANKED HALIBUT DINNER

| | |
|---|---|
| 4 halibut steaks, fresh or thawed frozen (about 2 lbs.) | ¼ teaspoon marjoram |
| | ½ teaspoon salt |
| | ⅛ teaspoon pepper |
| ¼ cup butter, melted | 2 large zucchini |
| 2 tablespoons olive oil | 1 pkg. (10 oz.) frozen green peas |
| 1 tablespoon wine vinegar | |
| 2 teaspoons lemon juice | 1 can (8¼ oz.) tiny whole carrots |
| 1 clove garlic, minced | Au Gratin Potato Puffs, *below* |
| ¼ teaspoon dry mustard | |

1.  Put halibut steaks into an oiled baking pan.
2.  Combine butter, olive oil, vinegar, lemon juice, garlic, dry mustard, marjoram, salt, and pepper. Drizzle over halibut.
3.  Bake at 450°F 10 to 12 minutes, or until halibut is almost done.
4.  Meanwhile, halve zucchini lengthwise and scoop out and discard center portion. Cook in boiling salted water until just tender.
5.  Cook peas following directions on package. Heat carrots.
6.  Prepare Au Gratin Potato Puffs.
7.  Arrange halibut on wooden plank or heated ovenware platter and border with zucchini halves filled with peas, carrots, and potato puffs. Dot peas and carrots with *butter*.
8.  Place platter under broiler to brown potato puffs. Sprinkle carrots with *chopped parsley*.
9.  Garnish with *sprigs of parsley* and *lemon wedges* arranged on a skewer.  4 SERVINGS

**AU GRATIN POTATO PUFFS:** Pare 1½ *pounds potatoes;* cook and mash potatoes in a saucepan. Add *2 tablespoons butter* and ⅓ *cup milk;* whip until fluffy. Add *2 slightly beaten egg yolks*, ½ cup

*shredded sharp Cheddar cheese, 1 teaspoon salt,* and *few grains pepper;* continue whipping. Using a pastry bag with a large star tip, form mounds about 2 inches in diameter on plank. Proceed as directed in recipe.

## BOUNDARY BAY CRAB BOUCHÉES

*This would be a good time — although any time is a good time — to try British Columbia's famous and unique Loganberry Wine.*

| | |
|---|---|
| ¼ cup butter | ½ cup shredded Cheddar cheese |
| ⅔ cup boiling water | |
| ½ cup all-purpose flour | 2 eggs |
| ¼ teaspoon salt | Crab Filling, *below* |

1.  Add butter to boiling water, then add flour and salt all at one time and stir together. Add cheese and stir again. Add the eggs, one at a time, and beat thoroughly after each addition.
2.  Drop by teaspoonfuls onto greased cookie sheets.
3.  Bake at 425°F 10 minutes, then reduce oven temperature to 350°F and bake 15 minutes longer.
4.  Split and fill with hot or cold crab filling.
ABOUT 6 SERVINGS

## CRAB FILLING

| | |
|---|---|
| 1 cup crab meat | 1½ teaspoons caraway seeds |
| ½ cup thinly sliced green onion | |
| | Mayonnaise to blend |
| 1 cup finely chopped celery | |

1.  Toss all ingredients lightly together in a bowl until thoroughly mixed.
2.  Heat in top of a double boiler over simmering water, or serve cold.  ABOUT 2 CUPS FILLING

NOTE: To serve as a salad, nestle filling in a *leaf of lettuce* and garnish with *pimiento* and *cucumber slices.*

## WEST COAST HALIBUT ROYALE

| | |
|---|---|
| 2 lbs. halibut steak | ½ cup chopped onion |
| Juice of 1 lemon | 2 tablespoons butter |
| 1 teaspoon salt | Green pepper strips |
| ½ teaspoon paprika | |

1.  Put fish steaks into a shallow dish. Mix lemon

juice, salt, and paprika; pour over fish. Marinate 1 hour, turning steaks over after first half hour.

2. Cook onion in butter until transparent.

3. Put steaks into a greased baking dish; top with onion and green pepper strips. Pour remaining butter over all.

4. Bake at 450°F 10 minutes per inch thickness of fish.                                  ABOUT 6 SERVINGS

## CREAMED OYSTERS DE LUXE

| | |
|---|---|
| 3 tablespoons butter or margarine | ½ teaspoon prepared mustard |
| ½ cup sliced fresh mushrooms | ⅛ teaspoon thyme |
| 1½ tablespoons grated onion | 1 cup cream |
| 1 tablespoon flour | ¾ pt. medium oysters, drained (reserve 2 tablespoons liquor) |
| ½ teaspoon salt | |
| ⅛ teaspoon white pepper | 2 tablespoons pimiento strips |
| Few grains cayenne pepper | |

1. Heat butter in a saucepan; add mushrooms and onion and cook until mushrooms are lightly browned, stirring occasionally. Remove mushrooms with a slotted spoon and set aside.

2. Blend a mixture of flour, salt, and peppers into the butter in saucepan; heat until mixture bubbles. Remove from heat and blend in mustard and thyme. Add cream and reserved oyster liquor gradually, stirring constantly. Continue to stir, bring to boiling, and boil 1 to 2 minutes.

3. Add oysters and cook over low heat 1 to 2 minutes, or until edges of oysters begin to curl. Remove from heat and stir in the pimiento and mushrooms.

4. Serve hot over *toasted buttered bread rounds* sprinkled with *ground nutmeg*.    ABOUT 6 SERVINGS

## LUNCHEON CRAB 'N' OYSTERS

| | |
|---|---|
| 2 tablespoons butter or margarine | 1 pkg. (6 oz.) frozen King crab, thawed |
| 2 tablespoons shredded Cheddar cheese | 2 doz. large oysters with liquor, bits of shell removed |
| ½ teaspoon salt | |
| 1 teaspoon Worcestershire sauce | 3 tablespoons butter or margarine |
| ¼ cup ketchup | 3 tablespoons flour |
| ¼ cup cream | |

1. Melt the 2 tablespoons butter and cheese in a double boiler over simmering water. Blend in salt, Worcestershire sauce, ketchup, and cream.

2. Add crab meat and oysters, including any liquid. Cook until edges of oysters begin to curl, about 10 minutes.

3. Drain mixture, reserving liquid. Set shellfish aside.

4. In top of double boiler over direct heat, melt the 3 tablespoons butter and blend in flour, browning very lightly. Gradually add liquid, stirring constantly. Bring to boiling and cook a few minutes. Stir in crab and oysters; heat over hot water.

5. Serve in heated *patty shells*.          6 SERVINGS

## SAUCE FOR SIMILKAMEEN ASPARAGUS
*Serve asparagus with drawn butter or with this sauce.*

| | |
|---|---|
| ¾ cup mayonnaise | Salt and pepper to taste |
| ⅓ cup milk | |
| 1 tablespoon lemon juice | Cooked fresh asparagus |

1. Cook mayonnaise and milk in the top of a double boiler over simmering water about 5 minutes. Mix in the lemon juice and seasonings.

2. Pour sauce over asparagus and garnish with *paprika* and *chopped parsley*.   ABOUT 1 CUP SAUCE

## OKAGAGAN SAVORY TOMATOES
*Rushed from market gardens daily during the season, delectable British Columbia tomatoes may be served sliced, with a pinch of powdered thyme or dill weed on each slice. Or, for a hot vegetable, try this recipe.*

| | |
|---|---|
| 8 large tomatoes | ⅛ teaspoon ground nutmeg |
| ½ cup finely chopped onion | ⅛ teaspoon powdered thyme |
| ¼ cup butter | |
| 3 tablespoons flour | ¼ teaspoon Worcestershire sauce |
| 1½ cups milk | |
| 1 teaspoon salt | 1 cup shredded Cheddar cheese |
| ¼ teaspoon pepper | |
| ⅛ teaspoon dry mustard | 1 cup soft bread crumbs |

1. To peel tomatoes, put each one into boiling water about ½ minute, or until skin loosens; slip off skin. Cut a slice off the top of each and scoop out the center pulp. Turn tomatoes upside down to drain.

2.   Sauté onion in butter until transparent. Blend in flour, then add milk and seasonings. Bring to boiling; cook and stir until thick. Stir in cheese and half the crumbs.

3.   Arrange tomatoes in a baking dish; fill with the sauce and sprinkle remaining crumbs over them.

4.   Bake at 375°F 20 minutes.          8 SERVINGS

## HERBED TOMATOES

| | |
|---|---|
| 4 medium firm ripe tomatoes | ¼ teaspoon salt |
| 2 teaspoons sugar | Few grains pepper |
| ¼ cup butter or margarine | 1 tablespoon tarragon vinegar |
| ½ clove garlic, crushed | ½ teaspoon dill weed |
| | ¾ cup snipped parsley |

1.   Remove stem ends from tomatoes and cut crosswise into halves. Place in a shallow baking pan. Sprinkle cut surfaces lightly with the sugar.

2.   Heat butter and garlic in a small skillet. Blend in remaining ingredients.

3.   Cover cut surfaces of tomato halves generously with butter-parsley mixture.

4.   Bake at 325°F about 10 minutes, or until heated through.          8 SERVINGS

NOTE: If desired, ¼ teaspoon basil and ¼ teaspoon thyme may be substituted for dill weed.

## SALMON SALAD MOLD

*The verdant hue of either asparagus or beans offers a pleasing color contrast to the pastel salmon mold.*

| | |
|---|---|
| ⅔ cup water | 1 jar (4 oz.) pimientos, drained and chopped |
| ⅓ cup lemon juice | 1 tablespoon finely chopped onion |
| 2 env. unflavored gelatin | |
| 1 can (15½ oz.) salmon | |
| 1 medium-sized cucumber, pared, seeds removed and discarded, and finely chopped (about 1 cup) | 2 teaspoons Worcestershire sauce |
| | ½ teaspoon salt |
| | 1 cup mayonnaise |
| ½ cup finely chopped green pepper | 1⅔ cups undiluted evaporated milk |

1.   Combine the water and lemon juice in a saucepan. Sprinkle the gelatin over the liquid to soften; stir over low heat until gelatin is dissolved. Remove from heat and set aside to cool.

2.   Remove skin and bones from salmon and flake

in its liquid. Blend salmon, cucumber, green pepper, pimientos, onion, Worcestershire sauce, and salt into the cooled gelatin. Stir in mayonnaise, then the evaporated milk until mixture is evenly blended.

3.   Turn into a 1½-quart mold. Chill until firm, 8 hours or overnight.

4.   Unmold onto chilled serving plate. Arrange *curly endive*, *tomatoes*, *radishes*, and *pickles* attractively around mold. Serve with *Caper Salad Dressing, below.*          6 TO 8 SERVINGS

## CAPER SALAD DRESSING

| | |
|---|---|
| ½ cup undiluted evaporated milk | 1 teaspoon salt |
| ½ cup salad oil | 1 tablespoon capers, drained |
| 2 to 3 tablespoons cider vinegar | |

Put all ingredients except the capers into an electric blender container. Blend until smooth and thickened. Stir in the capers. Chill thoroughly.

ABOUT 1 CUP DRESSING

## CELERY-PEAR SALAD

| | |
|---|---|
| 1 cup water | ¼ cup finely chopped onion |
| 1 cup sugar | 3 tablespoons salad oil |
| ¼ teaspoon vanilla extract | 2 tablespoons lemon juice |
| 3 firm ripe pears, halved, pared, and cored | ½ teaspoon sugar |
| 1 cup finely cut green celery | ¼ teaspoon crushed tarragon |
| | Pinch ground cinnamon |

1.   Mix water and sugar in a saucepan. Bring to boiling, stirring until sugar is dissolved. Cover; boil 5 minutes.

2.   Add extract and as many pear halves at a time as will fit in saucepan. Simmer about 5 minutes, or until pears are just tender. Remove pears with slotted spoon and put into a shallow dish.

3.   Meanwhile, parboil celery and onion for 1 minute in rapidly boiling *salted water*; drain.

4.   Spoon vegetables over pears and sprinkle lightly with *salt* and *pepper*.

5.  Pour a blend of the remaining ingredients over pears and vegetables; chill thoroughly.

6.  To serve, put each pear half onto a chilled individual salad plate lined with crisp *salad greens*. Spoon some of the dressing over each serving.

6 SERVINGS

## OGOPOGO APPLE DUMPLINGS

*If you* must *cook your apples, here is an old English recipe. We call them Ogopogo Apple Dumplings after the strange monster many people claim to have seen in Okagagan Lake, which runs down the valley famous for apple-growing.*

| | |
|---|---|
| 2 cups sugar | 2 cups all-purpose |
| 1 cup water | flour |
| ¼ teaspoon *each* | 2 teaspoons baking |
| ground cinnamon | powder |
| and nutmeg | ¼ teaspoon salt |
| ¼ cup butter | ¾ cup shortening |
| 6 firm apples | ½ cup milk |

1.  Combine sugar, water, cinnamon, and nutmeg in a saucepan. Heat until sugar is dissolved. Add butter and stir until melted.

2.  Pare apples; core and cut into eighths.

3.  Mix flour, baking powder, and salt; cut in shortening. Add milk and stir until a dough is formed.

4.  Roll out dough ¼ inch thick on a lightly floured surface and cut into 5-inch squares. Arrange 4 or 5 pieces of apple on each square; sprinkle with *sugar, cinnamon,* and *nutmeg*. Dot with *butter*. Fold corners to center and pinch edges together.

5.  Place dumplings 1 inch apart in a greased baking dish. Pour syrup over them.

6.  Bake at 325°F about 45 minutes.

7.  Serve hot with *cream*.       10 TO 12 DUMPLINGS

## BLUEBERRY MERINGUES

| | |
|---|---|
| 2 egg whites (about ⅓ | ½ cup sugar |
| cup) | ½ teaspoon ground |
| ½ teaspoon cream of | coriander |
| tartar | 1 cup fresh blueberries, |
| ½ teaspoon vanilla | rinsed and thoroughly |
| extract | drained |

1.  Combine egg white, cream of tartar, and vanilla extract; beat until frothy. Mix the sugar with coriander; add gradually to the egg whites, beating constantly until stiff peaks are formed. Fold in the blueberries.

2.  Drop by tablespoonfuls into mounds about 2 inches apart onto cookie sheet lined with baking parchment or other unglazed paper.

3.  Bake at 250°F about 1 hour, or until meringues are delicately browned and dry to the touch. Turn off oven and allow meringues to cool completely in oven (do not open oven door).

4.  Remove from paper.    ABOUT 2 DOZEN COOKIES

## SAANICH FRUIT PLATE

There are so many exquisite fruits in British Columbia that it is a shame to eat them any way but fresh. In addition to several varieties of apples, there are peaches, pears, apricots, strawberries, raspberries, blackberries, the unsurpassable Bing cherries and British Columbia's gift to the world — loganberries, which are a cross between raspberries and blackberries. A special delicacy, if you are lucky enough to get it, is wild blackberries. Smothered in Devonshire cream from Victoria, this is indeed a dessert to remember.

## PENTICTON PEACH PEAR CHILI SAUCE

*For something different in the way of relishes, try this using some of British Columbia's incomparable peaches and pears.*

| | |
|---|---|
| 15 medium tomatoes | 1 pt. vinegar |
| 3 large onions | 2 cups brown sugar |
| 4 peaches, peeled | ¼ cup whole mixed |
| 4 pears | spices (in a |
| 1 hot red pepper, finely | cheesecloth bag) |
| chopped | |

1.  Coarsely chop tomatoes, onions, peaches, and pears. Put into a large pot. Add red pepper, vinegar, brown sugar, and spices. Bring to boiling, reduce heat, and simmer gently 2½ hours, stirring occasionally. Remove spice bag.

2.  Ladle into sterilized jars, seal, and store in a cool place.       4 TO 5 PINTS CHILI SAUCE

# ALBERTA

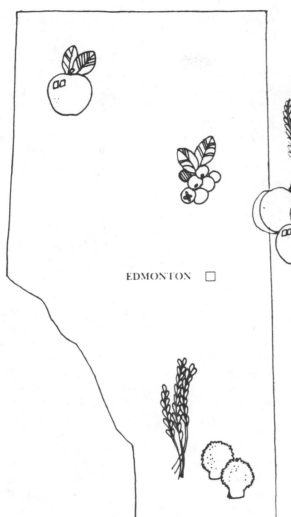

The rolling plains and foothills of Alberta make ideal pasture for cattle. Western beef is famous the world over, and Albertans think there is no food in the world to equal thick, rare, tender beef steaks. However, they have also produced two unusual beef dishes — Chuck Wagon Stew, named for the covered wagon used to take dinner to the cowhands on the range, and a form of beef mincemeat that is delectable in pies and tarts.

Alberta also produces succulent broad-breasted, grain-fed turkeys.

Ingenious use is made of wild fruits, flowers, and nuts, and recipes are given here for a wine, a cordial, a unique catsup, and nut bars.

Alberta is also a grain-growing area, and Alberta farmers take prizes year after year for their wheat at national and international agricul-

tural fairs. Using flour milled from this wheat, a very good cake has been created which is made in many homes to celebrate the New Year.

## CREAM OF NAVY BEAN SOUP

| | |
|---|---|
| 2 cups dried navy beans | 2 cups milk |
| 5 cups beef broth | 1 cup cream |
| 2 cups chopped onion | ½ teaspoon seasoned salt |
| 3 tablespoons butter or margarine | ¼ teaspoon pepper |
| 3 tablespoons flour | ¼ teaspoon paprika |

1. Wash beans and soak overnight in water to cover.
2. Drain beans and put into a large heavy saucepan. Add the broth and onion and mix well. Cover and simmer until beans are soft and mushy, about 1 hour.
3. Force bean mixture through sieve or food mill and set aside.
4. Heat butter in a large saucepan. Stir in the flour and cook until mixture bubbles and is lightly browned. Add the milk gradually, stirring

constantly; continue to stir and bring rapidly to boiling. Cook 1 to 2 minutes.

5. Stir in the bean purée, cream, and remaining ingredients. Heat thoroughly, stirring constantly.

6. Garnish with *minced parsley* and serve with generous amounts of *crumbled bacon* or *well-browned croutons*.   ABOUT 2 QUARTS SOUP

## VEGETABLE MEDLEY SOUP

| | |
|---|---|
| 8 slices bacon | 1 tablespoon salt |
| ½ cup chopped onion | 1 teaspoon sugar |
| ½ cup sliced celery | ¼ teaspoon pepper |
| 5 cups water | ¼ teaspoon crushed thyme or basil |
| 1½ cups fresh corn or 1 package (about 10 ounces) frozen corn | 1 cup fresh green beans, cut in 1-inch pieces |
| ½ cup sliced carrots | 4 cups chopped peeled tomatoes (4 to 5 tomatoes) |
| 1 potato, pared and sliced | |

1. Cook bacon until crisp in a Dutch oven or kettle. Drain off all but 2 tablespoons fat.

2. Sauté onion and celery in bacon fat.

3. Stir in water, corn, carrots, potato, salt, sugar, pepper, and thyme. Bring to boiling; simmer covered 30 minutes.

4. Stir in green beans; simmer 10 minutes, or until beans are crisp-tender

5. Stir in tomatoes; heat 5 minutes.

ABOUT 6 SERVINGS

## TUNNEL-OF-CARAMEL COFFEE CAKE

| | |
|---|---|
| ⅔ cup undiluted evaporated milk | 2 eggs, beaten |
| ¾ cup sugar | 5 cups all-purpose flour |
| ½ teaspoon salt | 2 pkgs. active dry yeast |
| ½ cup butter or margarine, softened | ½ cup warm water |
| | Caramel Filling, *below* |
| | Caramel Frosting, *below* |

1. Beat evaporated milk, sugar, salt, and butter together using an electric mixer. Add the beaten eggs and 2 cups of the flour; beat until smooth.

2. Soften yeast in the warm water. Add to the batter along with 1 cup of flour. Beat 3 minutes at medium speed.

3. Add remaining flour and beat until thoroughly mixed. Put into a greased deep bowl; turn dough to

bring greased surface to top. Cover; let rise in a warm place until doubled.

4. Punch down dough, turn onto a lightly floured surface, and knead until satiny smooth.

5. Roll dough into a 15x10-inch rectangle. Lightly brush with *melted butter or margarine* and spread with Caramel Filling. Roll up tightly starting with a long side. Place roll, open edge down, in a greased 10-inch tubed pan; join ends and press to seal. Cover; let rise in a warm place until doubled, about 2 hours.

6. Bake at 350°F 45 minutes. Remove from pan to a wire rack. Immediately ice with Caramel Frosting and decorate with *pecan halves*.

ONE 10-INCH COFFEE CAKE

CARAMEL FILLING: Mix *¼ cup melted butter or margarine, ⅔ cup lightly packed light brown sugar, and ⅔ cup flaked coconut.*

CARAMEL FROSTING: Blend *¼ cup lightly packed light brown sugar, 2 tablespoons undiluted evaporated milk, and 2 tablespoons melted butter or margarine. Add 1 cup sifted confectioners' (icing) sugar and beat until smooth.*

## DATE NUT BREAD

| | |
|---|---|
| ½ cup warm water | 5 to 5½ cups sifted all-purpose flour |
| 2 pkgs. active dry yeast | 1 cup whole wheat flour |
| 1¾ cups warm milk | 1 cup chopped dates |
| 2 tablespoons sugar | ½ cup chopped pecans |
| 1 tablespoon salt | 1 teaspoon ground cinnamon |
| 3 tablespoons margarine | |

1. Measure warm water into a warm large bowl. Sprinkle in yeast; stir until dissolved. Add warm milk, sugar, salt, and margarine. Stir in 2 cups all-purpose flour. Beat with rotary beater until smooth (about 1 minute). Add 1 cup all-purpose flour; beat with rotary beater until smooth (about 1 minute). Add 1 cup all-purpose flour; beat vigorously with a wooden spoon until smooth (about 150 strokes). Stir in whole wheat flour, dates, pecans, cinnamon, and enough of the remaining all-purpose flour to make a soft dough.

2. Turn dough onto a lightly floured surface. Knead 8 to 10 minutes, or until dough is smooth, elastic, and shows small blisters under surface when drawn tight. Cover with plastic wrap, then a towel. Let rest 20 minutes.

3. Punch dough down. Divide into 3 equal portions. Roll each into a 12x7-inch rectangle. Shape into loaves. Place in 3 greased 7x4x2-inch loaf pans. Brush loaves with *peanut oil*. Cover pans loosely with plastic wrap. Refrigerate 2 to 24 hours.

4. When ready to bake, remove loaves from refrigerator. Uncover dough carefully. Let stand uncovered 10 minutes at room temperature. Puncture with a greased wooden pick or metal skewer any gas bubbles which may have formed.

5. Bake at 400°F about 35 minutes. Remove from pans immediately, place on wire racks to cool, and, if desired, brush with margarine.

, 3 LOAVES BREAD

### FILBERT BREAD

| | |
|---|---|
| 1½ cups unblanched filberts | ½ cup butter or margarine |
| ½ cup sifted all-purpose flour | 2 teaspoons vanilla extract |
| ½ teaspoon baking powder | ½ cup plus 2 tablespoons sugar |
| ⅛ teaspoon salt | 2 eggs, well beaten |

1. Grate 1 cup of filberts and finely chop remaining nuts; mix together.

2. Sift flour, baking powder, and salt together; stir in nuts.

3. Cream butter and vanilla extract. Add sugar gradually, creaming until fluffy. Add eggs gradually, beating thoroughly. Beat in the dry ingredients only until well mixed. Turn batter equally into two greased 5x3x2-inch loaf pans and spread evenly.

4. Bake at 325°F 55 to 60 minutes.

5. Cool bread 15 minutes in pans on wire racks; remove from pans and cool completely before slicing or storing. 2 SMALL LOAVES BREAD

### SHORT RIBS, WESTERN STYLE

| | |
|---|---|
| 4 medium onions, quartered | 1 cup dried lima beans |
| 2 teaspoons salt | 2 lbs. lean beef short ribs |
| ¼ teaspoon pepper | 3 tablespoons flour |
| ½ teaspoon rubbed sage | 1 teaspoon dry mustard |
| 1 qt. water | 2 to 3 tablespoons fat |

1. Combine onions with salt, pepper, sage, and water in a heavy kettle; cover and simmer 5 minutes.

2. Add lima beans gradually to water so boiling does not stop. Simmer, uncovered, 2 minutes; remove from heat. Cover and set aside to soak 1 hour.

3. Meanwhile, coat short ribs evenly with a mixture of flour and dry mustard. Brown ribs on all sides in heated fat in a large skillet.

4. Add meat to lima beans in kettle; cover and simmer 1½ hours, or until beans and meat are tender. ABOUT 6 SERVINGS

### CHUCK WAGON STEW

| | |
|---|---|
| 1½ lbs. beef round steak | Salt and pepper to taste |
| 2 tablespoons flour | 12 small onions, peeled |
| 1 tablespoon shortening | 4 medium potatoes, diced |
| 4 cups boiling water | 2 cups sliced carrots |
| 1 bay leaf or ½ tablespoon vegetable bouquet sauce | 2 cups sliced apples |
| | 2 tablespoons butter or beef suet |

1. Cut steak into strips, roll in flour, and brown in shortening. Add boiling water and seasonings; simmer 2 hours.

2. Add vegetables, apples, and butter; simmer 1½ to 2 hours longer. ABOUT 6 SERVINGS

### SWEETGRASS BUFFALO AND BEER PIE

*Since buffalo are under control of the federal government and kept in special parks as a conservation project, buffalo meat is available only occasionally, when some of the animals are slaughtered. In the meantime, try the recipe with beef—it's almost just as good!*

| | |
|---|---|
| 4 lbs. buffalo meat | 2 pts. beef stock |
| Salt, pepper, and sage | 2 tablespoons tomato purée |
| Flour | 1 pt. beer |
| Oil | Herb bag (1 clove garlic, 1 bay leaf, parsley, 3 cloves, pinch of thyme) |
| 3 medium onions | |
| 3 carrots | |
| 3 stalks celery | |
| 3 potatoes | Pastry for 1-crust pie |
| 3 tablespoons flour | Milk |

1. Cut meat into 1-inch cubes and season with salt, pepper, and sage; roll in flour and brown in oil. Put meat into a heavy saucepan.

2. Cut vegetables in ½-inch cubes, sauté in the

same oil, and add to the meat. Add 3 tablespoons flour to the oil and let it brown. Add stock, tomato purée, and beer; blend. Add stock mixture and herb bag to meat and vegetables. Bring to boiling, reduce heat, and simmer until tender. Remove herb bag.

3. Turn stew into a casserole or individual pot pie dishes, cover with pastry, and brush with milk.

4. Bake, as directed in pastry recipe, until golden brown. 8 TO 12 SERVINGS

## BEEF KABOBS WITH PEACHES

6 canned peach halves
½ cup syrup drained from peaches
½ cup cooking or salad oil
¼ cup soy sauce
2 tablespoons lemon juice
2 tablespoons instant minced onion
1 teaspoon salt

Few grains black pepper
½ teaspoon ground ginger
1 clove garlic, crushed
1½ lbs. boneless beef sirloin steak, cut in 2-in. squares
12 cooked small whole onions
2 green peppers, cut in 2-in. squares

1. Mix thoroughly in a shallow dish the peach syrup, oil, soy sauce, lemon juice, minced onion, salt, pepper, ginger, and garlic. Add steak pieces and turn until pieces are coated. Refrigerate at least 2 hours, turning pieces several times. Remove meat from marinade and drain.

2. Thread meat pieces on 8-inch skewers alternately with onions and green pepper squares; put kabob pieces close together for rare meat, separate them slightly for well-done meat.

3. Arrange kabobs on broiler rack and brush with reserved marinade. Broil with tops of kabobs about 3 inches from source of heat, 7 to 10 minutes, turning kabobs several times; brush frequently with marinade. Test for doneness by cutting a slit in meat and noting internal color of meat.

4. During last 3 minutes of cooking, spear a peach half on the end of each skewer, brush with marinade and finish broiling. 6 SERVINGS

## CHICKEN OR TURKEY STUFFING

1 cup cornmeal
2 tablespoons baking powder
4 eggs
¼ cup milk
2 onions, diced

4 stalks celery, diced
3 tablespoons rendered chicken fat
½ teaspoon poultry seasoning

1. Combine cornmeal and baking powder. Make a well in the center of dry ingredients; add a mixture of 2 eggs, well beaten, and the milk. Beat until just smooth, being careful not to overmix.

2. Pour batter into a small greased iron skillet and cook on top of the range over medium heat until a wooden pick or cake tester inserted in center comes out clean.

3. When cornbread is done, fry onion and celery in hot chicken fat in a skillet until golden brown. Crumble cornbread and combine with onion mixture. Mix in remaining 2 eggs, fork beaten, and poultry seasoning; stuff prepared chicken or turkey.

ABOUT 3½ CUPS STUFFING

NOTE: This stuffing is also good baked in a casserole and served with your favorite meat gravy.

## TURKEY 'N' DRESSING BAKE

½ cup diced celery
¼ cup minced onion
3 tablespoons butter or margarine
3¼ cups chicken broth (dissolve 4 chicken bouillon cubes in 3¼ cups boiling water)
5 cups coarse whole wheat bread crumbs (reserve ½ cup crumbs for topping)

¼ cup snipped parsley
½ teaspoon salt
¼ teaspoon pepper
1 egg, slightly beaten
2 tablespoons flour
2 eggs, beaten
⅛ teaspoon pepper
¼ teaspoon crushed leaf sage
¼ teaspoon celery salt
Thin slices of cooked roast turkey

1. Cook celery and onion in hot butter in a large skillet about 5 minutes; combine with 1¾ cups of the chicken broth, 4½ cups bread crumbs, the parsley, salt, ¼ teaspoon pepper, and 1 egg. Mix lightly with a fork. Spoon the mixture over bottom of a 2-quart shallow baking dish; set aside.

2. In a saucepan, mix flour and ¼ cup cooled broth until smooth; heat until bubbly. Remove from heat and gradually add remaining broth, stirring constantly. Cook and stir over medium heat until

sauce comes to boiling; cook 2 minutes longer. Remove from heat and gradually add to eggs while beating. Blend in ⅛ teaspoon pepper, sage, and celery salt.

3. Arrange the desired amount of turkey over dressing in baking dish. Pour the sauce over all.

4. Toss reserved crumbs with about *1 tablespoon butter or margarine*; spoon over top.

5. Bake at 350°F 30 to 40 minutes, or until egg mixture is set. Garnish generously with snipped *parsley*. Accompany with *spiced peaches* and a relish tray of *ripe olives, radish roses,* and crinkle-cut *zucchini strips*.          6 SERVINGS

## TURKEY ROYAL

¼ cup butter or margarine
1 tablespoon minced onion
6 tablespoons flour
1 teaspoon salt
Few grains cayenne pepper
Few grains ground nutmeg
Milk
2 cans (5 oz. each) button mushrooms, drained (reserve liquid)
3 egg yolks, slightly beaten
2 cups dairy sour cream
1 tablespoon minced parsley
1 tablespoon minced chives
¼ cup pimiento strips
½ cup cooked green peas
2 cups cooked turkey pieces

1. Heat the butter in top of a double boiler. Add the onion and cook until onion is transparent. Blend in flour, salt, cayenne pepper, and nutmeg. Heat until bubbly.

2. Add enough milk to mushroom liquid to make 1 cup. Gradually add liquid to saucepan with butter mixture, stirring constantly. Bring to boiling; cook and stir 1 to 2 minutes.

3. Vigorously stir about 3 tablespoons of the hot mixture into egg yolks. Immediately blend into mixture in double boiler. Cook and stir over simmering water 5 to 10 minutes, or until thoroughly heated.

4. Vigorously stir sour cream, in very small amounts, into hot mixture. Mix in parsley, chives, pimiento, peas, mushrooms, and turkey. Heat thoroughly over simmering water.

5. Serve plain or on *toast points, hot biscuits,* or fluffy *cooked rice*.          6 SERVINGS

## APPLE-STUFFED ACORN SQUASH

2 acorn squash
2 tart apples
1½ teaspoons grated lemon peel
1 tablespoon lemon juice
¼ cup butter or margarine, melted
⅓ cup firmly packed brown sugar
Salt
Cinnamon

1. Cut squash into halves lengthwise and scoop out seedy centers. Place cut side down in baking dish and pour in boiling water to a ½-inch depth. Bake at 400°F 20 minutes.

2. Pare, core, and dice apples; mix with lemon peel and juice, 2 tablespoons butter, and brown sugar.

3. Invert squash halves and brush with remaining 2 tablespoons butter; sprinkle with salt and cinnamon.

4. Fill squash halves with apple mixture. Pour boiling water into dish to a ½-inch depth; cover and bake 30 minutes.

5. Before serving, spoon pan juices over squash. If desired, garnish with *apple* and *lemon slices*.          4 SERVINGS

## COUNTRY-STYLE BAKED BEANS

6 cups water
1 lb. dried navy beans, washed and sorted
2 teaspoons salt
½ teaspoon pepper
1 large clove garlic, chopped
1 bay leaf
12 slices bacon
2 medium onions, chopped
1 medium green pepper, chopped
3 medium ripe tomatoes, peeled and chopped
¼ cup chopped parsley
½ teaspoon oregano

1. Bring water to boiling in a saucepot, add beans, and boil 2 minutes. Cover; remove from heat and let stand 1 hour. Add salt, pepper, garlic, and bay leaf. Cook, covered, over low heat until beans are tender but not mushy, about 2 hours. Drain; reserve liquid.

2. Meanwhile, fry bacon until crisp; reserve ¼ cup bacon fat. Drain bacon and crumble.

3. Return reserved bacon fat to skillet, add onion and cook, stirring occasionally, until light golden. Stir in green pepper and tomatoes; cook 5 minutes. Blend in parsley and oregano. Combine with beans; add bacon pieces and toss mixture lightly with a fork to blend thoroughly.

4. Turn mixture into a bean pot or casserole and add bean liquid to cover.

5. Bake, uncovered, at 350°F 1 to 1½ hours, adding liquid if necessary.    8 TO 10 SERVINGS

## WHIPPED YAMS IN SHELLS

| | |
|---|---|
| 4 medium-sized yams, baked | 1¼ teaspoons grated lemon peel |
| ½ teaspoon salt | 2 tablespoons lemon juice |
| ½ teaspoon ground nutmeg | 3 tablespoons honey |
| ¼ teaspoon ground ginger | 2 tablespoons butter or margarine |

1. Slit potato peel; scoop out centers and reserve shells intact. Whip yam pulp with remaining ingredients.

2. Fill reserved shells with yam mixture and set on a baking sheet. Heat in a 350°F oven about 20 minutes.

3. Garnish with *lemon slices* and sprigs of *parsley*.    4 SERVINGS

## DATE LAYER CAKE

| | |
|---|---|
| ¾ cup (about 5 oz.) dates, finely chopped | 2 cups sifted all-purpose flour |
| 1 cup boiling water | 1 teaspoon baking soda |
| ⅓ cup lightly packed brown sugar | ½ cup butter |
| ¼ cup granulated sugar | 1 cup granulated sugar |
| ½ cup pecans, coarsely chopped | 1 egg |

1. Put dates into a small bowl. Cover with the boiling water. Set aside.

2. Mix brown sugar, ¼ cup granulated sugar, and pecans. Set aside for topping.

3. Sift flour and baking soda together; set aside.

4. Cream butter; add remaining granulated sugar gradually, creaming until fluffy. Add egg and beat thoroughly.

5. Beating only until smooth after each addition, alternately add dry ingredients in fourths and date mixture in thirds to creamed mixture. Turn batter into 2 prepared 8-inch layer cake pans and spread evenly to edges. Sprinkle brown sugar topping evenly over batter in one pan only.

6. Bake at 350°F 30 to 35 minutes, or until cake tests done.

7. Cool and remove from pans. Put together with a *cream filling* using crumb-topped layer for top.

ONE 8-INCH 2-LAYER CAKE

## DOUBLE-CHOCOLATE NUT LOAF CAKE

| | |
|---|---|
| 1¾ cups sifted cake flour | 4 oz. (4 sq.) unsweetened chocolate, melted and cooled |
| 2 teaspoons baking powder | 1 cup milk |
| ¾ cup butter or margarine | 4 egg whites |
| 1 teaspoon vanilla extract | ¾ cup sugar |
| ¾ cup sugar | 1 cup chopped pecans |
| 4 egg yolks, well beaten | 1 oz. (1 sq.) unsweetened chocolate, grated |

1. Sift the cake flour and baking powder together; set aside.

2. Cream butter with extract. Gradually add ¾ cup sugar, creaming until fluffy. Add the egg yolks in thirds, beating well after each addition. Blend in the cooled chocolate.

3. Beating only until smooth after each addition, alternately add dry ingredients in fourths and milk in thirds to creamed mixture.

4. Beat egg whites until frothy. Gradually add ¾ cup sugar, continuing to beat until stiff peaks are formed. Gently fold batter into meringue until thoroughly blended. Fold in pecans and grated chocolate. Turn batter into 2 prepared 8x4x2-inch loaf pans.

5. Bake at 325°F 55 to 60 minutes, or until cake tests done.

6. Remove from oven to wire rack and cool 15 minutes before removing from pans. Cool completely.    TWO 8x4-INCH LOAF CAKES

## PIONEER'S NEW YEAR CELEBRATION CAKE

| | |
|---|---|
| ⅔ cup butter | 1 cup milk |
| 1 teaspoon vanilla extract | 2 teaspoons sugar |
| 1 cup sugar | ¼ cup blanched almonds |
| 3 eggs, well beaten | 12 candied cherries, cut in halves |
| 2¼ cups cake flour | |
| 1 tablespoon baking powder | |

1. Cream butter, vanilla extract, and 1 cup sugar. Add eggs gradually, beating thoroughly.

2. Mix cake flour and baking powder. Add to creamed mixture alternately with milk.

3. Turn into a greased 9x5x3-inch loaf pan and spread to corners. Sprinkle with 2 teaspoons sugar and decorate with almonds and cherries.

4. Bake at 400°F 15 minutes, at 375°F 15 minutes, and at 350°F 25 minutes. ONE 9x5-INCH LOAF CAKE

## BUTTERNUT PUMPKIN PIE

| | |
|---|---|
| 1⅓ cups fine graham cracker crumbs | ½ teaspoon ground cinnamon |
| ⅓ cup lightly packed brown sugar | ¼ teaspoon ground ginger |
| ⅓ cup butter, melted | ¼ teaspoon ground nutmeg |
| 1 cup cooked pumpkin | 1 qt. butter pecan ice cream |
| ½ cup granulated sugar | Sweetened whipped cream |
| ¼ teaspoon salt | Pecan halves |

1. Mix crumbs and brown sugar. Add melted butter and mix thoroughly. Press evenly into a 9-inch pie pan. Chill.

2. Combine pumpkin, granulated sugar, salt, and spices.

3. Turn ice cream into a large bowl; beat with electric mixer to soften. Fold pumpkin mixture into ice cream. Spoon into chilled shell. Freeze until firm.

4. Garnish pie with whipped cream and pecans. ONE 9-INCH PIE

## OLD-FASHIONED PEACH COBBLER

| | |
|---|---|
| 1 cup lightly packed brown sugar | 2½ teaspoons baking powder |
| 4 teaspoons cornstarch | ½ teaspoon salt |
| 6 cups sliced fresh peaches | ⅓ cup chilled butter |
| 3 whole cloves | 1 teaspoon grated lemon peel |
| 1 piece (3 in.) stick cinnamon | ¾ cup milk |
| 1½ cups sifted all-purpose flour | 1¼ cups light cream |
| 3 tablespoons granulated sugar | 2 tablespoons brandy (optional) |

1. Combine brown sugar and cornstarch in a saucepan. Stir in peaches, cloves, and cinnamon. Cook over medium heat, stirring constantly, until mixture is clear and comes to boiling. Cover and continue to cook over low heat 5 minutes, stirring

occasionally. Remove spices. Cover and keep warm.

2. Sift flour, granulated sugar, baking powder, and salt together into a bowl. Cut in butter until particles are fine. Add lemon peel and milk; mix lightly with a fork until just combined. Bring fruit mixture to boiling and pour into a 2-quart shallow baking dish. Drop tablespoonfuls of batter onto fruit mixture, spacing evenly.

3. Bake at 400°F about 30 minutes.

4. Pour cream (mixed with brandy, if desired) over individual servings of warm cobbler.

6 TO 8 SERVINGS

## GOLDEN HARVEST HAZELNUT COOKIES

| | |
|---|---|
| 1 cup butter | 2½ cups ground hazel-nuts (filberts can be used) |
| 1 cup sugar | |
| 2 eggs | |
| 1 cup flour | 1 egg, beaten (for brushing) |

1. Cream butter and sugar. Add eggs, one at a time, and beat thoroughly after each addition. Mix in flour and nuts. Chill thoroughly, preferably overnight.

2. Shape mixture into bars about 3 inches long, 1 inch wide, and ½ inch thick. Brush with beaten egg.

3. Arrange on greased cookie sheets.

4. Bake at 350°F 10 to 15 minutes. Cool cookies on wire rack. ABOUT 3 DOZEN COOKIES

## OLD-FASHIONED VANILLA SUGAR COOKIES

| | |
|---|---|
| Vanilla Sugar, *below* | 1 tablespoon vanilla extract |
| 4 cups sifted all-purpose flour | 2 cups sugar |
| 1 teaspoon baking soda | 2 egg yolks |
| 1 teaspoon salt | 1 cup buttermilk |
| 1 cup shortening | 2 egg whites |

1. Have Vanilla Sugar ready.

2. Sift flour, baking soda, and salt together.

3. Beat shortening with vanilla extract in a large

bowl. Add sugar gradually, creaming thoroughly. Beat in egg yolks until mixture is light and fluffy.

4. Alternately add dry ingredients in fourths and buttermilk in thirds to creamed mixture, beating only until blended after each addition.

5. Using a clean beater, beat egg whites until stiff (not dry) peaks are formed. Fold into batter until blended.

6. Drop about 2 tablespoons batter for each cookie onto greased baking sheets, spacing batter 3 inches apart. Using the back of a spoon, spread and shape each into a 2½-inch round ½ inch high. Sprinkle generously with Vanilla Sugar.

7. Bake at 375°F about 15 minutes, or until browned around the edges. Immediately remove to wire racks and sprinkle again with Vanilla Sugar.

ABOUT 2½ DOZEN COOKIES

VANILLA SUGAR: Pour *2 pounds granulated sugar* into a container having a tight-fitting cover. Split a *vanilla bean* in half lengthwise, then cut into 1-inch pieces. Poke pieces down into the sugar at irregular intervals. Cover container tightly and store. The longer the sugar stands, the richer the vanilla flavor. Stir in additional sugar as sugar is used. If tightly covered, sugar may be stored for several months.

## ALBERTA MINCEMEAT

*Use to make unusual and zestful meat pies and tarts.*

| | |
|---|---|
| 14 cups chopped cooked beef | 3 lbs. currants |
| 3 cups chopped suet | 3 lbs. raisins |
| 28 cups chopped apples | ½ lb. mixed citrus peel |
| 3 qts. boiled cider | 1 qt. boiling water |
| 2 qts. molasses | 8 oz. ground cinnamon |
| 10 lbs. sugar | 2 oz. ground cloves |
| | 8 oz. ground coriander |

1. Combine all ingredients in a very large kettle. Cook until apples are soft.

2. Ladle mixture into sterilized jars, seal, and store in a cool place.

## COOKING LAKE ROSE HIP CATSUP

*Rose hips are sometimes called "Alberta oranges" because they have a very high vitamin C content.*

| | |
|---|---|
| 4 qts. ripe rose hip berries | ½ tablespoon *each* celery seed, whole allspice, mace, and cloves |
| 2 medium onions, sliced | |
| 1 clove garlic | |
| 1 cup water (more if necessary) | Stick cinnamon (2 inches) |
| ¾ cup brown sugar | 1 cup vinegar |

1. Boil berries, onions, garlic, and water until soft. Strain. Add brown sugar to strained mixture. Tie spices in a cheesecloth bag and add. Bring to boiling; add vinegar and boil 10 minutes.

2. Ladle mixture into sterilized jars, seal, and store in a cool place.

## FORT SASKATCHEWAN CHOKECHERRY CORDIAL

| | |
|---|---|
| Chokecherries | Sugar |
| Vinegar | |

1. Wash very ripe berries and put them through a food chopper or electric blender; turn into a crock and add vinegar just to cover. Let stand 8 days.

2. Strain mixture through a cheesecloth bag. Measure juice and add 1 cup sugar to each cup juice. Heat and stir until sugar is dissolved.

3. Bottle liquid and let stand a week or two before using. It will keep indefinitely.

4. To serve, put about ½ inch of juice in the bottom of a glass and fill with ice water.

## MEDICINE HAT DANDELION WINE

| | |
|---|---|
| 4 qts. dandelion blossoms (no stems) | 2 lemons |
| | 1 orange |
| 4 qts. sugar | 1 cake compressed yeast |
| 4 qts. boiling water | |

1. Put dandelion blossoms into a stone jar or crock. Add sugar, then boiling water.

2. Grate peel and squeeze juice from lemons and orange. When dandelion mixture is lukewarm, stir in grated peel and juice, then yeast. Cover and let stand 24 hours.

3. Strain mixture through a fine cloth and let stand 3 days. Strain again and let it ferment. When fermenting action ceases, bottle liquid.

# SASKATCHEWAN

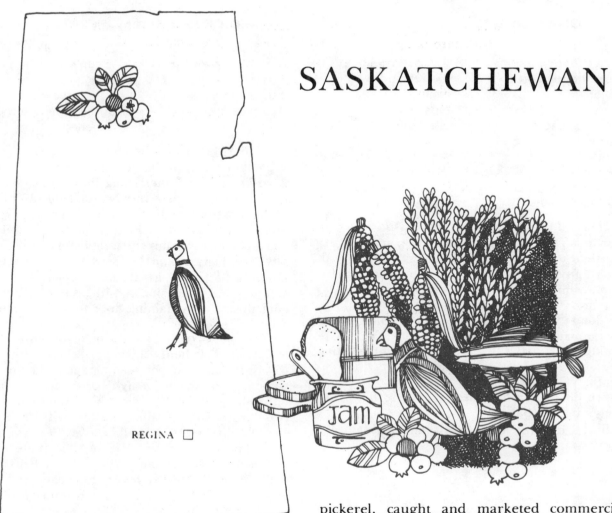

REGINA □

In the southern half of Saskatchewan, golden vistas of rippling grain beautify the late summer landscape, for here are grown wheat, oats, barley, rye, and other grains on huge farms, some of them two, three, or more square miles in extent. Early settlers used some of the flour milled from Saskatchewan wheat to make bannock, a kind of bread made without yeast or shortening and with long-keeping qualities. If no oven was available, it would be baked in an iron pot placed on hot coals, with the embers raked up round it. To this day there are many families who make bannock. To eat a slice of it hot from the oven, slathered in butter with homemade wild strawberry jam, is a heart-warming experience.

The northern half of Saskatchewan abounds in lakes and woods, and from it come whitefish and pickerel, caught and marketed commercially, some in Indian cooperatives. Not on sale, but available to every fisherman who even half tries, is the delicately flavored lake trout, which grows to trophy size in the cold, northern waters.

Many native wild berries grow in this province and are used for jellies, jams, cordials, pies, and puddings. One is the saskatoon, which looks like a blueberry but has its own unique flavor, and another is the pincherry with which a tart, tangy jelly can be made that can't be compared with anything else. Perfect with wild game!

Saskatchewan has another claim to the gourmet's attention: over it two of the continent's main migration channels converge, causing one of the highest concentrations of migratory birds in the world. Partridge and prairie chicken are especially popular, so a recipe for baked partridge has been included, in case you are lucky enough to be offered one or to shoot one yourself.

## SEAFOOD BISQUE

¼ cup butter
¼ cup chopped onion
⅓ cup chopped green onion
2 cups chicken broth
1 cup chopped celery
3 carrots, cut in small pieces
1 teaspoon salt
⅛ teaspoon pepper
¼ teaspoon thyme

2 bay leaves
½ lb. frozen halibut, thawed and cut in small pieces
3 cups milk
⅓ cup flour
1 cup light cream
1 pkg. (6 oz.) frozen crab meat, thawed
1 can (7½ oz.) minced clams

1. Heat butter in a large saucepan. Add onion and green onion and cook until soft.
2. Stir in the chicken broth, celery, carrots, salt, pepper, thyme, bay leaves, and halibut. Simmer about 25 minutes, or until vegetables and fish are just tender.
3. Blend 1 cup milk with the flour. Slowly pour into the saucepan, stirring constantly. Mix in remaining milk and the cream. Continue stirring, bring to boiling, and cook until mixture is thick and smooth.
4. Stir in the crab meat and clams; heat thoroughly. Remove bay leaves.
5. Serve in large soup bowls and garnish with *sprigs of parsley.*          ABOUT 8 SERVINGS

## CHILLED CHERRY SOUP

⅓ cup sugar
1 tablespoon cornstarch
½ cup water
2 cans (14 oz. each) pitted tart red cherries

1 cinnamon stick
3 cloves
2½ cups milk
Few drops red food coloring (optional)

1. Combine sugar and cornstarch in a saucepan. Stir in water, cherries with liquid, cinnamon, and cloves. Bring to boiling over medium heat, stirring occasionally until thickened and clear. Cover and cook over low heat 3 to 5 minutes, stirring as necessary.
2. Cool, then chill well. Remove cinnamon and cloves. Add milk gradually to chilled mixture, stirring constantly. Tint with food coloring, if desired.
3. Serve soup well chilled.          ABOUT 7 CUPS SOUP

## RAISED CORNMEAL MUFFINS

5 to 5¼ cups sifted all-purpose flour
½ cup sugar
1 tablespoon salt
2 pkgs. active dry yeast

2¼ cups milk
½ cup shortening
2 eggs
1 cup yellow cornmeal
Butter or margarine, melted

1. Mix 2¾ cups flour, sugar, salt, and undissolved yeast thoroughly in a large mixer bowl.
2. Put milk and shortening into a saucepan. Set over low heat until very warm (120-130°F). Add liquid mixture gradually to dry ingredients while mixing until blended. Beat 2 minutes at medium speed of electric mixer, scraping bowl occasionally. Mix in eggs and 1¾ cups flour, or enough to make a batter. Beat at high speed 2 minutes, scraping bowl occasionally. Blend in cornmeal and enough of the remaining flour to make a smooth, thick batter.
3. Cover; let rise in a warm place until double in bulk (1 to 1½ hours).
4. Beat batter down. Cut against side of bowl with a large spoon enough batter at one time to fill each greased 2½- or 3-inch muffin-pan well two-thirds full, pushing batter with a rubber spatula directly into well. Cover; let rise again until almost double in bulk (about 30 minutes).
5. Bake at 400°F about 20 minutes. Brush tops with melted butter. Remove from pans and serve piping hot.          1½ TO 2 DOZEN MUFFINS

## BRAN ROLLS

¾ cup whole bran cereal
⅓ cup sugar
1½ teaspoons salt
½ cup margarine
½ cup boiling water
½ cup warm water

2 pkgs. active dry yeast
1 egg, beaten
3¼ to 3¾ cups sifted all-purpose flour

1. Combine bran cereal, sugar, salt, and margarine in a bowl. Add boiling water; stir until margarine is melted. Cool to lukewarm.
2. Measure warm water into a warm large bowl. Sprinkle in yeast; stir until dissolved. Mix in lukewarm cereal mixture, egg, and enough of the flour to make a stiff dough.
3. Turn dough onto a lightly floured surface;

knead 8 to 10 minutes, or until smooth and elastic. Form dough into a ball and place in a greased deep bowl; turn to bring greased surface to top. Cover; let rise in a warm place until double in bulk (about 1 hour).

4.  Punch dough down; divide in half. Divide each half into 12 equal pieces. Form each piece into a small ball. Place in greased muffin-pan wells, 2½x1½ inches, or in 2 greased 8-inch round cake pans. Brush rolls with *melted margarine*. Cover; let rise again until double in bulk (about 30 minutes).

5.  Bake at 375°F 20 to 25 minutes. Remove from pans and place on wire racks. Serve warm.

2 DOZEN ROLLS

## BANNOCK

2¾ cups all-purpose flour

2 teaspoons baking powder

½ teaspoon salt

3 tablespoons lard

⅔ cup water (about)

1.  Blend flour, baking powder, and salt in a bowl. Cut in lard with a pastry blender or 2 knives until particles are fine. Add water gradually, stirring with a fork until a soft, slightly sticky dough is formed.

2.  Turn dough out onto a lightly floured surface and knead gently 8 to 10 times. Roll out or pat to ½-inch thickness. Put onto a lightly greased baking sheet.

3.  Bake at 450°F 12 to 15 minutes, or until light golden brown. Serve hot with *butter*.      1 LOAF BREAD

## BLUEBERRY MUFFINS

2 cups all-purpose flour

¼ cup sugar

4 teaspoons baking powder

½ teaspoon salt

2 tablespoons butter

1 cup milk

2 eggs, beaten

1 cup blueberries

Flour

1.  Mix flour, sugar, baking powder, and salt. Work in butter. Add milk and eggs; mix.

2.  Mix blueberries with a small amount of flour; fold into batter.

3.  Spoon batter into greased muffin-pan wells.

4.  Bake at 425°F 25 minutes.

ABOUT 1 DOZEN MUFFINS

## WHEAT GERM MUFFINS

1 cup sifted all-purpose flour

4 teaspoons baking powder

¼ teaspoon baking soda

½ teaspoon salt

1 cup toasted wheat germ

2 tablespoons soft butter

¼ cup lightly packed brown sugar

1 egg

1 teaspoon grated orange peel

¼ cup orange juice

¾ cup plain yogurt

1.  Sift flour, baking powder, baking soda, and salt; mix in wheat germ.

2.  Cream butter with brown sugar. Add egg and beat well. Beat in orange peel and orange juice.

3.  Add dry ingredients alternately with yogurt to creamed mixture, mixing lightly after each addition.

4.  Fill greased medium muffin-pan wells about ¾ full.

5.  Bake at 425°F about 15 minutes. Serve warm with butter.      ABOUT 1 DOZEN MUFFINS

## TURKEY-OYSTER CASSEROLE

*Here's a tempting combination of turkey and oysters specially appropriate for holiday buffet entertaining.*

1 tablespoon butter

2 teaspoons grated onion

4 oz. fresh mushrooms, sliced lengthwise

¼ cup butter

¼ cup flour

1 teaspoon salt

¼ teaspoon black pepper

Few grains cayenne pepper

2 cups milk

1 egg yolk, slightly beaten

2 tablespoons chopped parsley

¼ teaspoon thyme

2 drops Tabasco

2 cups diced cooked turkey

1 pt. oysters (with liquor), heated just to boiling and drained

Buttered soft bread crumbs

1.  Heat the 1 tablespoon butter with the onion in a skillet; add mushrooms and cook over medium heat until lightly browned, stirring occasionally. Set aside.

2.  Heat the ¼ cup butter in a saucepan over low heat. Stir in the flour, salt, and peppers; cook until bubbly. Add the milk gradually, stirring until well blended. Bring rapidly to boiling and boil 1 to 2 minutes, stirring constantly.

3.  Blend a small amount of the hot sauce into **egg**

yolk and return to sauce, stirring until mixed.
4. Stir in parsley, thyme, and Tabasco. Add the turkey, oysters, and mushrooms; toss lightly until thoroughly mixed.
5. Turn mixture into a buttered 1½-quart shallow baking dish. Sprinkle with the crumbs.
6. Heat in a 400°F oven about 10 minutes, or until mixture is bubbly around edges and crumbs are golden brown. ABOUT 6 SERVINGS

## PILE O' BONES TURKEY

Pile o' bones is the English meaning of the Cree word *Wascana*, which was the original name of the city of Regina, the provincial capital. Pile o' bones is also what is left when you serve meaty, broad-breasted Saskatchewan turkey. Traditional accompaniments to roast turkey are mashed potatoes, mashed turnips, new or frozen green peas, and cranberry sauce or jelly. Here is a good and unusual stuffing for the turkey.

## TURKEY STUFFING

| | |
|---|---|
| 8 slices fresh bread, grated | 2 tablespoons butter, melted |
| 3 cups salted peanuts, finely chopped or crushed | 1 egg, beaten |
| ½ cup dry wine | 1 teaspoon poultry seasoning |
| ½ cup chicken broth | Pepper to taste |

Mix bread and peanuts. Combine wine, broth, butter, egg, and seasonings. Toss dry mixture with a fork while adding liquid mixture. Stuff lightly into cavities of turkey. Roast as directed.
ENOUGH STUFFING FOR AN 8-POUND TURKEY

## HANSON LAKE PICKEREL

| | |
|---|---|
| 2 lbs. pickerel fillets | ¼ cup lemon juice |
| Salt and pepper | 2 tablespoons chopped fresh or dried mint |
| ¼ cup melted butter or salad oil | |

1. Sprinkle fish with salt and pepper; put on rack in a broiler pan.
2. Mix butter, lemon juice, and mint. Brush generously over fish.
3. Broil about 5 inches from heat 5 minutes. Turn, brush again with butter mixture, and broil 5 minutes, or until cooked. Garnish with *lemon slices*.
ABOUT 6 SERVINGS

## CABBAGE ROLLS PAPRIKASH

| | |
|---|---|
| 8 large cabbage leaves | ½ teaspoon salt |
| 2½ cups diced cooked chicken | ½ teaspoon thyme leaves |
| 2 tablespoons chopped onion | 1 egg, beaten |
| ½ cup finely chopped celery | 2 tablespoons butter or margarine |
| ¼ lb. chopped fresh mushrooms | 6 tablespoons flour |
| 1 small clove garlic, minced | 2 cups chicken broth |
| | 2 cups dairy sour cream |
| | 3 tablespoons paprika |

1. Cook cabbage leaves 4 minutes in boiling salted water to cover. Drain and pat dry.
2. Mix chicken, onion, celery, mushrooms, garlic, salt, and thyme; stir in egg.
3. Place ½ cup of the chicken mixture in the center of each cabbage leaf. Fold sides of the cabbage leaf toward center, over filling, and then fold and overlap ends to make a small bundle. Fasten with wooden picks. Place in a 3-quart baking dish.
4. Heat butter in a large skillet. Blend in flour and heat until bubbly. Add chicken broth gradually, stirring until smooth. Blend in sour cream and paprika. Cook over low heat, stirring constantly, until thickened. Pour sauce over cabbage rolls. Cover baking dish.
5. Cook in a 350°F oven 35 minutes. 4 SERVINGS

## BAKED PARTRIDGE IN SHERRY

| | |
|---|---|
| 2 partridge | 1 tablespoon chopped celery |
| ½ small onion, chopped | 1 teaspoon salt |
| 1 clove garlic, minced | ¼ teaspoon pepper |
| ⅓ cup butter | ½ cup sherry |

1. Cut birds, using breasts and thighs. Brown lightly with onion and garlic in butter. Put in roasting pan, add celery, salt, pepper, and sherry. Cover pan.
2. Bake at 350°F 1½ hours; baste frequently, adding water if necessary. 4 SERVINGS

## LAC LA RONGE LAKE TROUT

1 lake trout (3 lbs.), skinned, boned, and filleted
1 cup corn flakes, crushed
1 medium onion, sliced
Salt
Pinch *each* garlic powder and thyme
3 fresh tomatoes, cut in pieces, or 1 can (19 oz.) tomatoes, drained
¼ cup water
Butter
Paprika

1. Put trout fillets into a greased baking dish. Mix corn flakes, onion, seasonings, tomatoes, and water (or ¼ cup liquid from canned tomatoes). Dot with butter and sprinkle with paprika.
2. Bake at 450°F 10 minutes per inch thickness of fish.

4 TO 6 SERVINGS

## SEAFOOD-RICE MEDLEY
*Tart apples add a unique touch to this scallop, shrimp, and rice casserole — hearty food for hungry appetites.*

1 lb. scallops, rinsed in cold water
1 teaspoon salt
1 large onion, sliced
2 cloves garlic, finely chopped
6 whole cloves
12 peppercorns
2 teaspoons caraway seed
1 lb. small fresh shrimp
2 tablespoons butter or margarine
2 tablespoons chopped onion
3 medium tart red apples, washed, cored, and diced
¼ cup lemon juice
¼ cup firmly packed light brown sugar
3 cups warm cooked rice
½ cup salted almonds, coarsely chopped
1 can (10 oz.) condensed cream of celery soup

1. Pour 1 quart boiling water over scallops and salt in a saucepan. Cook, covered, until scallops are just tender. Remove from stock with a slotted spoon. Cut scallops into halves; set aside.
2. To the stock, add sliced onion, garlic, cloves, peppercorns, and caraway seed. Simmer, covered, about 10 minutes.
3. Meanwhile, rinse shrimp under running cold water; remove shells and devein shrimp. Bring stock to boiling; add shrimp and simmer, covered, 3 to 5 minutes, or until shrimp are plumped and turn pink. Drain in a colander; reserve 1⅓ cups of the stock. Remove shrimp from colander, with

some of the caraway seeds adhering to them. Discard the remaining spices.
4. Spoon scallops and shrimp equally into 8 buttered individual casseroles; set aside.
5. Heat butter in a large heavy skillet. Add chopped onion and cook about 3 minutes. Add apples and drizzle with lemon juice and brown sugar; toss mixture to blend.
6. Remove from heat. Add the cooked rice and almonds; toss lightly with a fork to blend thoroughly. Spoon mixture into the casseroles.
7. Stir the reserved stock into soup; bring to boiling, stirring frequently. Pour over mixture in casseroles.
8. Set in 350°F oven about 25 minutes, or until thoroughly heated.

8 SERVINGS

## HERBED SHRIMP SKILLET

¼ cup butter or margarine
½ cup chopped onion
½ cup diced green pepper
3 cups fresh-cut corn (about 5 ears)
2 medium tomatoes, peeled and diced
2 teaspoons sugar
1 teaspoon salt
¼ teaspoon freshly ground pepper
¼ teaspoon basil
¼ teaspoon crushed thyme
2 cans (4¼ oz. each) shrimp, drained and rinsed

1. Heat butter in a heavy skillet. Add onion and green pepper and cook until almost tender, about 5 minutes, stirring occasionally to cook evenly.
2. Mix in corn and tomatoes. Blend sugar, salt, pepper, basil, and thyme; stir in. Bring to boiling and cook, covered, about 5 minutes, or until corn is tender.
3. Stir in shrimp and heat thoroughly.

ABOUT 6 SERVINGS

## QU'APPELLE VALLEY CORN ON THE COB
"Qu'appelle" means "who calls?" When you call family and friends to a corn roast, they'll come a-running. The important thing about corn is that it be sweet corn, grown for human consumption, rather than feed corn. Next in importance is its freshness, for the natural sugar in the corn becomes converted to starch as time goes on. Corn should be eaten before it is 8 hours off the stalk. The third important feature is that it not be overcooked. Corn on the cob should be boiled no more

than 10 minutes, so that the edible kernels are still tasty and crunchy, not soggy and tasteless. Only the kernels need cooking; the cobs are discarded. Fresh, sweet, shucked corn, boiled 10 minutes, rolled in melted butter, sprinkled with salt and pepper, mounted on corn picks at either end, or held in the fingers, is so deservedly popular that it might almost be called a national dish.

## CORN ROAST

Until you have sat on a sandy beach with the music of water lapping at your feet, before you a glowing bonfire and above you a golden harvest moon, and in your hands a piping hot cob of corn from which you munch the sweet and succulent kernels, you just haven't lived a full life!

Pull back the husks and remove the silks from *fresh corn*. Then soak the cob, husks and all, in cold water for 20 to 30 minutes. This ensures that the husks are wet through. Drain the cobs, dry them, brush them with *melted butter* and tie the husks back in place. Roll each cob up in a piece of aluminum foil, sealing it tightly. Place the corn in the glowing coals of the bonfire and let it roast, turning several times, for 20 to 30 minutes, depending on the size of the cob. Shuck the corn, add *salt* and *pepper* and more *melted butter*, if desired, and start getting the next round ready!

## CORN SPOON BREAD

| | |
|---|---|
| 1 qt. milk | 2 teaspoons salt |
| 1 cup yellow cornmeal | 1 teaspoon sugar |
| 2 tablespoons finely chopped onion | 1 teaspoon baking powder |
| 2 tablespoons chopped parsley | ¼ teaspoon pepper |
| 4 eggs | 2 cups corn kernels (fresh, frozen, or canned) |
| 2 tablespoons butter or margarine | |

1.　Scald milk in top of a double boiler over simmering water.
2.　Add cornmeal to scalded milk gradually, stirring constantly. Mix in onion and parsley. Cook over boiling water until thickened, about 10 minutes, stirring frequently and vigorously.
3.　Meanwhile, beat eggs in a large bowl until thick and piled softly.

4.　Remove double boiler top from water. Stir in butter. Blend salt, sugar, baking powder, and pepper; stir into cornmeal mixture. Add hot mixture gradually to eggs, beating constantly. Mix in corn. Turn into a buttered 2-quart casserole.
5.　Bake at 425°F 40 to 45 minutes, or until top is browned. Serve immediately.　6 TO 8 SERVINGS

## BAKED STUFFED TOMATOES WITH CORN

| | |
|---|---|
| 6 medium firm ripe tomatoes | ¼ teaspoon celery salt |
| Salt | ¼ teaspoon marjoram |
| 1 egg, fork beaten | ¼ teaspoon thyme |
| ¼ cup minced onion | Few grains pepper |
| ¼ cup minced green pepper | ¾ cup buttered fine dry bread crumbs |
| 1 cup whole kernel corn | |

1.　Cut out stem ends of tomatoes. Cut a slice from top of each tomato. Scoop out pulp with a spoon and finely chop; set aside. Sprinkle inside of tomato shells with salt and set in a shallow baking dish.
2.　Mix into egg the reserved tomato pulp, onion, green pepper, corn, celery salt, marjoram, thyme, pepper, and ¼ cup bread crumbs. Spoon mixture into tomato shells. Top with remaining crumbs.
3.　Bake at 400°F about 15 minutes, or until thoroughly heated.　6 SERVINGS

## HUNGARIAN CHERRY TORTE

| | |
|---|---|
| Torte: | 2 cans (14 oz. each) dark sweet cherries, drained, cut in halves, and drained thoroughly |
| ⅔ cup blanched almonds, grated | |
| ¼ cup fine dry bread crumbs | |
| 6 egg yolks (about ½ cup) | Meringue: |
| ⅓ cup sugar | 3 egg whites |
| 3 tablespoons lemon juice | 6 tablespoons sugar |
| 6 egg whites (⅞ cup) | Topping: |
| 3 tablespoons sugar | ¼ cup blanched almonds, toasted and coarsely chopped |
| | 2 tablespoons sugar |

1.　For torte: Blend the grated almonds and bread crumbs. Divide into four portions; set aside.
2.　Put the egg yolks, ⅓ cup sugar, and lemon juice into a small bowl. Beat until very thick; set aside.

3. Using a clean bowl and beater, beat the egg whites until frothy. Add the 3 tablespoons sugar gradually, continuing to beat until stiff peaks are formed.

4. Gently fold egg yolk mixture and 1 portion of the crumb mixture into beaten egg whites until batter is only partially blended. Repeat with remaining crumb mixture, folding in one portion at a time. Finally, fold just until blended; do not overmix.

5. Turn batter into an ungreased 9-inch springform pan and spread evenly to edges. Gently place cherries, cut side down, evenly over top.

6. Bake at 350°F about 40 minutes, or until torte tests done.

7. Set on wire rack; cool in pan 15 minutes. Remove only the side section of the pan; cool torte completely.

8. For meringue: Using a clean bowl and beater, beat the egg whites until frothy. Add the sugar gradually, continuing to beat until stiff peaks are formed.

9. Transfer torte to a baking sheet. Completely cover sides and top of torte with the meringue. Mix topping ingredients together and sprinkle evenly over top of meringue.

10. Bake at 350°F 10 to 15 minutes, or until meringue is delicately browned.

11. Cool torte and transfer to a cake plate. Before cutting, dip knife blade into hot water; wipe blade after each cut.

ONE 9-INCH TORTE

## SASKATOON PIE
*Luscious served with whipped cream.*

| | |
|---|---|
| Pastry for a 2-crust 9-in. pie | 2 tablespoons flour or 1 tablespoon cornstarch |
| 4 cups saskatoons | ⅛ teaspoon salt |
| 1 tablespoon fresh lemon juice | ⅛ teaspoon *each* ground cinnamon and cloves |
| 1 cup sugar | |

1. Prepare pastry.
2. Wash saskatoons, toss with lemon juice, and turn into unbaked pie shell. Mix sugar, flour, salt, and spices. Pour over saskatoons. Dot with *butter.* Cover with top crust.
3. Bake at 425°F 10 minutes, then reduce temperature to 350°F and bake 25 to 30 minutes.

ONE 9-INCH PIE

## CHERRY-RHUBARB PIE

| | |
|---|---|
| 1 can (14 oz.) pitted tart red cherries (water packed), drained | ⅛ teaspoon baking soda |
| 1 lb. fresh rhubarb, sliced about ⅛ in. thick | ½ teaspoon almond extract |
| 1¼ cups sugar | Few drops red food coloring |
| ¼ cup quick-cooking tapioca | Pastry for a 2-crust 9-in. pie |

1. Mix cherries, rhubarb, sugar, tapioca, baking soda, almond extract, and red food coloring; let stand 20 minutes.
2. Prepare pastry. Roll out enough pastry to line a 9-inch pie pan; line pie pan. Roll out remaining pastry for top crust and slit pastry with knife in several places to allow steam to escape during baking.
3. Pour filling into pastry-lined pan; cover with top crust and flute edge.
4. Bake at 450°F 10 minutes. Reduce oven temperature to 350°F and bake 40 to 45 minutes. Remove from oven and set on a wire rack. Serve warm or cooled.

ONE 9-INCH PIE

## HOMESTEADERS' PANCAKES WITH PINCHERRY JELLY
*The usual way to eat these is to butter them lavishly, then add maple syrup, corn syrup, or brown sugar. But Westerners often eat them with a jelly made from wild berries.*

| | |
|---|---|
| 2 eggs | 1 cup all-purpose flour |
| ½ cup sugar | 2½ teaspoons baking powder |
| ½ cup evaporated milk | |
| ½ cup water | 1 teaspoon ground nutmeg |
| 1 teaspoon vanilla extract | ½ teaspoon salt |

1. Beat eggs and add sugar, evaporated milk, water, and vanilla extract; beat well. Mix flour, baking powder, nutmeg, and salt; add to liquid mixture and beat until blended.
2. Drop batter by spoonfuls onto a lightly greased hot griddle; turn when batter begins to bubble.
3. Serve with Pincherry Jelly.

1 TO 2 DOZEN PANCAKES

## PINCHERRY JELLY

Wash *pincherries*, add *water to cover*, and simmer until soft. Drain through a cheesecloth bag. Measure the juice and for each cup of juice measure ¾ cup of *sugar*; place the sugar in the oven to get warm. Simmer the juice until a clot forms when it is dropped from a spoon. Add the heated sugar and simmer until the jelly sheets from a spoon. Pour into sterilized jars and seal. There is no need to use commercial pectin with pincherries — they have plenty of their own.

## CARAMEL CRUNCH PUDDING

Pudding:
1½ cups sugar
½ cup boiling water
3 tablespoons cornstarch
1½ cups milk
1 egg, slightly beaten
1 teaspoon vanilla
    extract
1 tablespoon butter
½ cup whipping cream

Crunch mixture:
¼ cup lightly packed
    brown sugar
¼ cup all-purpose
    flour
¼ cup quick-cooking
    rolled oats
¼ cup finely chopped
    pecans
¼ cup soft butter

1.   For pudding, measure 1¼ cups sugar into a heavy saucepan. Heat, stirring constantly until melted and golden. Remove from heat and add boiling water very carefully while stirring. Return to heat and bring to boiling.
2.   Combine cornstarch and milk. Add gradually to caramel syrup, stirring constantly. Bring to boiling over medium heat, stirring occasionally. Cover and cook over low heat 3 to 5 minutes; stir as necessary. Stir a small amount of hot mixture with egg. Blend with mixture in saucepan. Cook 2 minutes, stirring constantly. Add vanilla extract and butter. Cover and cool. Chill.
3.   Whip cream until soft peaks are formed; beat in remaining ¼ cup sugar. Fold into pudding. Chill.
4.   For crunch mixture, combine brown sugar, flour, oats, pecans, and butter; mix until crumbly. Press mixture lightly into an 8-inch square pan.
5.   Bake at 350°F 12 to 15 minutes. Crumble into small pieces. Cool.
6.   To serve, spoon alternate layers of pudding and crunch mixture into sherbet or parfait glasses.

**6 TO 8 SERVINGS**

## ORANGE GLAZED DATE BARS

1½ cups sifted all-
    purpose flour
¾ teaspoon baking
    soda
½ teaspoon salt
¾ cup lightly packed
    brown sugar
1¼ cups (8 oz.)
    chopped pitted dates

½ cup water
½ cup soft butter
3 eggs, slightly
    beaten
½ cup milk
½ cup orange juice
1 cup chopped pecans
Orange Glaze, *below*

1.   Sift flour, baking soda, and salt together.
2.   Combine brown sugar, dates, and water in a large saucepan. Cook over medium heat, stirring constantly until dates soften. Remove from heat and stir in butter. Add eggs and mix well.
3.   Add dry ingredients to date mixture; stir until blended. Add milk and orange juice gradually, mixing well. Stir in nuts.
4.   Bake at 350°F about 30 minutes.
5.   Cool completely in pan on wire rack. Spread glaze over top and cut into bars.

**3 TO 4 DOZEN COOKIES**

**ORANGE GLAZE:** Combine *2 tablespoons soft butter, 1½ cups sifted confectioners' (icing) sugar, 1½ teaspoons grated orange peel, and 2½ tablespoons orange juice*; beat until smooth.

## OATMEAL DROP COOKIES

2 cups sifted all-
    purpose flour
1 cup sugar
1 teaspoon baking soda
1 teaspoon ground
    cinnamon
½ teaspoon salt
1 cup shortening

1 cup chopped nuts
2½ cups uncooked
    rolled oats
½ teaspoon grated
    lemon peel
3 eggs, well beaten
½ cup milk

1.   Mix flour, sugar, baking soda, cinnamon, and salt in a bowl. Cut in shortening with a pastry blender or two knives until pieces are the size of rice kernels. Mix in nuts, oats, and lemon peel. Add eggs gradually, mixing thoroughly. Mix in milk thoroughly.
2.   Drop by teaspoonfuls about 2 inches apart onto cookie sheets.
3.   Bake at 375°F about 10 minutes, or until delicately browned. Cool on wire racks.

**ABOUT 7½ DOZEN COOKIES**

# MANITOBA

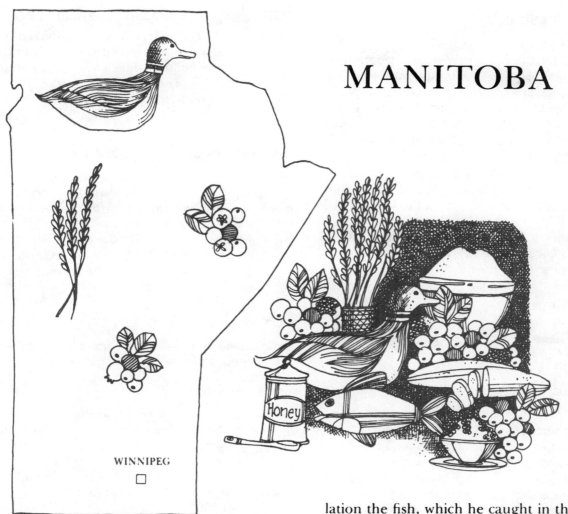

WINNIPEG
□

Manitoba has several unique claims to fame in the gourmet's lexicon. One is the famous Winnipeg goldeye, a delicate fish processed in an unusual way. They are smoked over oak logs and then dyed a deep coral. They are usually served whole, one to a person, for they average about three quarters of a pound, and make a very attractive plate when garnished with lemon wedges and parsley. The processing was originated in the early 1890s by a young English butcher who found his Winnipeg store was having indifferent success and was forced to turn to nocturnal fishing to augment his income.

The young Englishman, Robert Firth, constructed a makeshift smokehouse from a barrel in which to cure his catches. Through a miscalculation the fish, which he caught in the Red River at Winnipeg, became more than half cooked instead of merely smoked. The result of this "mistake" was the smoked Winnipeg goldeye.

Wild rice, although it is also found in northern Ontario, is best known in Manitoba. To harvest the grain, Indians pole their canoes through the shallow marshes, bending the stalks inward and beating the heads.

Three of the four major North American flyways pass over Manitoba and wild game is abundant. Many kinds of fish are also found and, while whitefish is caught in all the inland provinces, Selkirk whitefish is especially well known.

We have included a recipe for hot biscuits made from flour milled from Manitoba wheat. Other dainties for which Manitoba is famous are caviar and honey. And, of course, there are the wild berries from which piquant jellies are made.

## PARTY CHEESE LOG

2 cups grated sharp
Cheddar cheese (8 oz.)
1 pkg. (4 oz.) pimiento
cream cheese
¼ cup crumbled blue
cheese
⅓ cup mayonnaise or
salad dressing
½ teaspoon
Worcestershire sauce
½ teaspoon chili powder
½ teaspoon onion salt
Chopped parsley,
chopped nuts, sesame
seed, or paprika

1. Cream Cheddar, cream, and blue cheeses together in a bowl. Blend in mayonnaise, Worcestershire sauce, chili powder, and onion salt. Chill if necessary.
2. Shape into a long roll; coat as desired. Wrap in aluminum foil and chill overnight.
3. Slice cheese log and serve with *crackers*.

1 CHEESE LOG (ABOUT 3 DOZEN SLICES)

## FRESH VEGETABLE BEEF SOUP

Beef broth:
3 tablespoons butter
or margarine
3 lbs. beef shank
cross cuts
1 clove garlic, peeled
2 onions, peeled and
cut in pieces
4 pieces celery with
leaves
4 tomatoes, cut in
wedges
2 carrots, pared and
cut in pieces
1 bay leaf
1½ teaspoons thyme
leaves
2 parsley sprigs
4 beef bouillon cubes
6 peppercorns
1 tablespoon salt
4½ qts. water
Vegetables for soup:
1½ cups sliced celery
1½ cups sliced
pared carrots
3 cups chopped cabbage
2 cups fresh green
beans, cut in 1-in.
pieces
4 tomatoes, peeled and
chopped
4 large potatoes, pared
and cut in 1-in. cubes
1½ cups fresh corn
kernels
1 tablespoon salt

1. For broth, heat butter in a large kettle. Add beef shank and brown on all sides. Add garlic, onions, celery, tomatoes, carrots, herbs, bouillon cubes, peppercorns, salt, and water. Cover; bring to boiling, reduce heat, and simmer about 2 hours.
2. Remove meat. Strain broth and return broth to kettle. Cut meat into small pieces and add to broth.
3. For soup, add celery, carrots, cabbage, green beans, tomatoes, potatoes, corn, and salt to broth. Cover; bring to boiling, reduce heat, and simmer 30 minutes, or until vegetables are tender.
4. Ladle hot soup into bowls.

ABOUT 5½ QUARTS SOUP

## CAVIAR ON JELLIED CONSOMMÉ

Simmer *beef soup bones* in *water*, seasoned with *salt, pepper*, a *bay leaf*, a *pinch of savory*, a *pinch of garlic, sliced onions*, and *2 thin slices of lemon*, for 2 hours. Strain and measure. For each two cups of broth mix in 1 envelope of *unflavored gelatin*. Serve broken up by spoonfuls, garnish with a topping of *sour cream* and *Manitoba caviar*.

## HOT BISCUITS AND MANITOBA HONEY

2 cups cake flour
2½ teaspoons baking
powder
1 teaspoon salt
4 tablespoons butter
or shortening
¾ cup milk

1. Mix cake flour, baking powder, and salt; cut in butter. Add milk and stir with a fork until a dough is formed. Knead dough gently until completely blended.
2. Roll out dough to ¼-inch thickness. Cut with a biscuit cutter. Put onto ungreased baking sheet.
3. Bake at 450°F 12 to 15 minutes.
4. Serve piping hot with *butter* and *Manitoba honey*.

ABOUT 1½ DOZEN BISCUITS

## BANANA BRAN BISCUITS

1⅓ cups sifted
all-purpose flour
2 tablespoons sugar
1 tablespoon baking
powder
½ teaspoon baking
soda
1 teaspoon salt
1 cup whole bran cereal
½ cup chilled butter
½ cup dairy sour cream
½ cup mashed ripe
banana
¼ cup milk

1. Mix flour, sugar, baking powder, baking soda, and salt in a bowl. Stir in bran. Add butter and cut in with pastry blender or 2 knives until pieces are fine.
2. Combine sour cream, banana, and milk. Add

to dry ingredients and mix lightly with a fork until flour is moistened.

3. Turn dough onto an ungreased baking sheet. Pat into a square about ¾ inch thick. Mark with a knife into 12 squares.

4. Bake at 450°F about 15 minutes. Serve warm with Honey Butter.                    1 DOZEN BISCUITS

## HONEY BUTTER

½ cup butter                    ⅓ cup honey

Beat butter until light and fluffy. Add honey gradually while beating. Pile into a small serving dish.

ABOUT 1 CUP BUTTER

## PARSLEYED OVEN POT ROAST

1½ teaspoons salt
¼ teaspoon pepper
1 beef round bottom round roast (4½ to 5 lbs.)
1 can (28 oz.) tomatoes, cut in pieces
¾ cup dry red wine
¼ cup instant minced onion
½ teaspoon instant minced garlic
2 tablespoons parsley flakes
1 bay leaf
1 teaspoon salt
6 medium carrots, pared and sliced
1½ lbs. zucchini, sliced
2 cups cherry tomatoes, pricked with fork

1. Rub 1½ teaspoons salt and the pepper over surface of meat.

2. Place meat, fat side down, in a heavy oven-proof casserole or Dutch oven. Brown well on all sides in a 450°F oven (about 1 hour). Drain off fat.

3. Combine tomatoes, wine, onion, garlic, parsley flakes, bay leaf, and salt. Pour over meat. Cover; reduce oven temperature to 350°F and cook 2 hours. Mix in carrots and cook 30 minutes, then mix in zucchini and cook 20 minutes. Finally, mix in cherry tomatoes and continue cooking 10 minutes, or until meat and vegetables are tender.

4. Serve meat and vegetables on a heated platter.
8 TO 10 SERVINGS

NOTE: If desired, serve pot roast with Old-Fashioned Cauliflower Pickles (page 64) and mashed potatoes topped with chives.

## SELKIRK WHITEFISH

Whitefish is excellent stuffed and baked. The fish should be washed and dried, and the backbone removed. Stuff it loosely, allowing about 1 cup of stuffing for each pound of dressed fish. Fasten the opening with skewers or wooden picks laced up with string. Place it on an oiled pan, brush it with oil and bake at 450°F for 10 minutes per inch thickness of fish measured at its thickest part.

## FISH STUFFING

½ cup chopped onion
½ cup chopped green pepper
½ cup chopped celery
3 tablespoons butter
3 cups soft bread crumbs
½ teaspoon poultry or Italian seasoning
Salt and pepper
¼ cup tomato juice

Sauté vegetables in butter until tender. Mix with bread crumbs, seasonings, and tomato juice.

## WINNIPEG GOLDEYE

Many people claim that the only way to cook *goldeye* is to season it and broil it for 10 minutes on each side, basting it liberally with *butter*. Another method is to place each *goldeye* on a greased sheet of aluminum foil, add *salt* and *pepper* and *butter*, fold the foil up and seal it completely, and bake it at 450°F for 10 minutes for each inch of thickness. This is one fish that needs no sauce or stuffing to confuse its own delicate flavor.

## LAKE WINNIPEGOSIS WILD DUCK

*Wild ducks* are much smaller than domestic ones, so they are seldom stuffed. Instead their cavities are sprinkled with *salt* and *pepper*, and alternate *thick slices of onion and orange* are placed inside. Some cooks sprinkle a little ginger in, too. The ducks are best cooked on a rack in a covered roasting pan at 350°F for 45 minutes, then finished uncovered for 30 minutes. Cold *applesauce* or *grape jelly* is traditionally served with them.

## WILD RICE

| | |
|---|---|
| 1 cup wild rice | 1 tablespoon chopped |
| 1 qt. water | pimiento |
| ½ lb. fresh mushrooms | ½ cup butter |
| 2 sprigs celery leaves, | ½ teaspoon Italian |
| chopped | seasoning |
| ½ green pepper, diced | Pinch thyme |
| 1 medium onion, | Salt and pepper |
| chopped | ½ cup chicken or |
| 1 tablespoon chopped | beef broth |
| parsley | |

1. Wash wild rice and combine with water; simmer about 1 hour. Drain.
2. Sauté vegetables in butter and add seasonings and broth; mix well. ABOUT 6 SERVINGS

NOTE: This is better made the day before, as it gives the flavors time to blend. It can be heated in the top of a double boiler and will keep until you are ready to eat it.

## CREAMED SPINACH

| | |
|---|---|
| 1 tablespoon butter | ¾ teaspoon seasoned |
| 1 pkg. (12 oz.) frozen | salt |
| chopped spinach, | 1 teaspoon grated onion |
| partially defrosted | 1 tablespoon flour |
| | ½ cup dairy sour cream |

1. Heat butter in a heavy skillet. Add spinach, seasoned salt, and onion. Cover and cook over high heat 1 to 2 minutes. Reduce heat and cook 5 minutes, stirring occasionally.
2. Sprinkle flour over spinach and blend in. Add sour cream in very small amounts, stirring until blended. Heat about 2 minutes but do not boil. Sprinkle with *paprika*. ABOUT 4 SERVINGS

## ASSINIBOINE JELLIED CUCUMBER SALAD

*Manitoba produces exceptionally good vegetables, among them firm, flavorful cucumbers.*

| | |
|---|---|
| 1 pkg. lime-flavored | 1 cup dairy sour cream |
| gelatin | or 1 cup mayonnaise |
| ¾ cup boiling water | or half of each |
| ¼ cup lemon juice | 1 cup chopped |
| 1 teaspoon onion juice | cucumber |

1. Dissolve gelatin in boiling water. Add lemon and onion juice. Chill until slightly thickened. Mix sour cream or mayonnaise or both and cucumber into gelatin.
2. Turn into a 1-quart mold. Chill until firm.
3. Unmold salad and garnish with *strips of green pepper and pimiento.* ABOUT 6 SERVINGS

## CUCUMBERS IN SOUR CREAM

| | |
|---|---|
| 1 large cucumber, rinsed | 1 tablespoon chopped |
| and pared | chives |
| ½ cup dairy sour cream | ¾ teaspoon salt |
| 1½ tablespoons cider | ⅛ teaspoon white |
| vinegar | pepper |

1. Score cucumber ⅛ inch deep by drawing the tines of a fork lengthwise over entire surface, then cut into thin slices.
2. Combine remaining ingredients and pour over the cucumber slices; toss lightly to coat evenly. Chill mixture thoroughly.
3. Serve garnished with finely chopped *hard-cooked egg yolk.* ABOUT 1 CUP RELISH

## AUTUMN APPLE PIE

| | |
|---|---|
| 1 can (19 oz.) apple | 2 eggs |
| pie filling | 1 teaspoon vanilla |
| 1 unbaked 9-in. pie | extract |
| shell | ½ teaspoon ground |
| 2 pkgs. (4 oz. each) | cinnamon |
| soft cream cheese | ½ teaspoon ground |
| ⅓ cup sugar | nutmeg |

1. Spoon pie filling into shell.
2. Cream cheese until light and fluffy. Add sugar gradually, beating constantly. Add eggs, one at a time, beating well after each addition. Add vanilla extract and spices. Pour over apples.
3. Bake at 375°F 35 to 40 minutes, or until topping is set. Cool. ONE 9-INCH PIE

## RED RIVER WILD CRANBERRY JELLY

*Wild cranberries* should be picked just before they are absolutely ripe if they are to be used for jelly-making. Wash the berries, cover with *water* and simmer until tender. Strain through cheesecloth. Measure liquid and add an equal amount of *sugar.* Simmer until jelly will sheet from a spoon. Put into sterilized jars and seal.

# ONTARIO

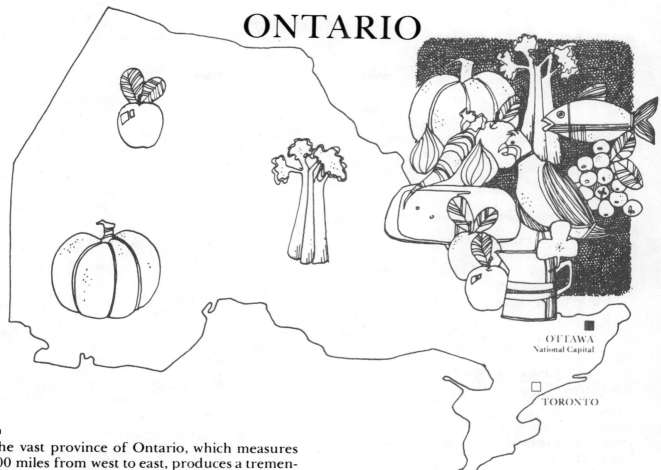

OTTAWA
National Capital

□ TORONTO

The vast province of Ontario, which measures 1,000 miles from west to east, produces a tremendous variety of food and has happily incorporated into its cuisine the culinary arts of the many immigrants who have brought their cooking secrets with them. In the "banana belt" of southwestern Ontario, orchards burst into spectacular bloom in the spring, harbingers of luscious crops of fruit, both large and small, to come. Here also are extensive market gardens, and even soy beans and tobacco are grown in Ontario's "sun-parlor."

From its three-quarters of a million lakes come a variety of delicious fish, among them whitefish, pike, lake trout, and the delicately flavored smelt. At Parry Sound, on Georgian Bay, a gala smelt fry is held in the streets at the peak of the season. Arctic char is not native to the province (it is in the Yukon and the Northwest Territories), but the commercially sold char, caught and marketed by Eskimo cooperatives, is reasonably easy to buy in Ontario. The Eskimo calls it Ilkaluk and it is such a superb fish that we had to include a recipe.

Ninety percent of the wine produced in Canada comes from vineyards of Ontario. It is much less expensive than imported wine, yet compares favorably in flavor and body.

Ontario is also famous for its cheese, and it would be hard to refute its claim that it makes the best Cheddar in the world. Particularly since World War II it has expanded its cheese production into new fields, and you can now buy almost any kind of cheese—Danish, Dutch, Swiss, French, English—produced in Ontario.

Ontario is a happy hunting-ground for fishermen and hunters, so it seemed a good idea to include a recipe for pheasant.

There are a great many food-processing plants in Ontario, among them plants producing pasta products. Macaroni mousse makes unusually good use of a pasta and also provides an opportunity to use another locally processed, local food —frozen mixed vegetables.

Last but not least, there is a 17th-century recipe for making honey without bees—that works!

## ROASTED CHEESE CANAPÉS

*This recipe dates back to 1847, at least, probably long before. It can be served in large pieces as a luncheon treat as well as an appetizer with Ontario wines.*

| | |
|---|---|
| 1 cup (4 oz.) grated aged Cheddar cheese | ¼ teaspoon salt |
| 6 tablespoons butter | ¼ teaspoon dry mustard |
| 2 egg yolks, slightly beaten | ⅛ teaspoon paprika |
| 1 teaspoon Worcestershire sauce | 1 cup soft bread crumbs |
| | 6 slices toast, crusts removed |

1. Combine all ingredients, except toast, and beat until smooth.
2. Spread 3 tablespoons of mixture on each slice of toast and broil until bubbly, about 3 minutes.
3. Cut in fancy shapes and serve immediately.

ABOUT 3 DOZEN CANAPÉS

## PIQUANT CHEESE LOAF

| | |
|---|---|
| 7 to 7¼ cups sifted all-purpose flour | 6 eggs (at room temperature) |
| 1 teaspoon sugar | ½ lb. Muenster cheese, shredded (about 2 cups) |
| 1 tablespoon salt | |
| 2 pkgs. active dry yeast | 2 cups julienne cooked ham (optional) |
| 1 cup plain yogurt | |
| ½ cup water | 1 egg, slightly beaten |
| 2 tablespoons margarine | 1 tablespoon milk |

1. Mix 1½ cups flour, sugar, salt, and undissolved yeast thoroughly in a large mixer bowl.
2. Combine yogurt, water, and margarine in a saucepan. Set over low heat until very warm (120–130°F); margarine does not need to melt. Add liquid mixture gradually to dry ingredients while beating at low speed of electric mixer. Beat at medium speed 2 minutes, scraping bowl occasionally. Add 6 eggs, 1 cup flour, and 1½ cups shredded cheese. Beat at high speed 2 minutes, scraping bowl occasionally. Stir in enough of the remaining flour to make a stiff dough.
3. Turn dough onto a lightly floured surface. Knead 8 to 10 minutes, or until dough is smooth, elastic, and shows small blisters under surface when drawn tight.
4. Form dough into a ball and place in greased deep bowl; turn to bring greased surface to top.

Cover; let rise in a warm place until double in bulk (about 1 hour).
5. Punch down dough; turn onto lightly floured surface. Divide in half. If using ham, knead 1 cup ham strips into each half. Shape each half into a ball and place on a greased cookie sheet. Cover; let rise again until double in bulk (about 1 hour).
6. Combine egg and milk; brush over loaves. Sprinkle with remaining ½ cup cheese.
7. Bake at 350°F about 30 minutes. Remove from cookie sheets and place on wire racks to cool.

2 LOAVES BREAD

## SKILLET BEEF STEW WITH NOODLES

| | |
|---|---|
| ¼ cup olive oil | ½ teaspoon crushed red pepper |
| 3 small onions, sliced | |
| 3 lbs. lean beef for stew, cut in 1½- in. pieces | 1 cup beef broth |
| | 1 can (16 oz.) tomatoes, drained |
| 3 cloves garlic, minced | |
| 2 teaspoons salt | 2 green peppers, cut in pieces |
| ½ teaspoon oregano | |

1. Heat oil in a large skillet; add onions and cook until tender, stirring occasionally; remove onions with a slotted spoon to a bowl.
2. Add the meat to skillet and brown evenly over medium heat, stirring occasionally.
3. Mix garlic with the salt; add to skillet along with onions, oregano, red pepper, and broth. Bring to boiling; cover and simmer 2 hours, or until meat is almost tender.
4. Add the tomatoes and cut into pieces with a spoon. Stir in green pepper, cover and cook about 15 minutes longer.
5. Serve with *buttered noodles*. ABOUT 8 SERVINGS
NOTE: For those who prefer uncooked green pepper and extra crunch, reserve ½ cup of the green pepper pieces and mix in just before serving.

## STUFFED MINI-ROLLS

| | |
|---|---|
| 12 chicken thighs, boned* | Apple-Raisin Stuffing, *below* (or use 12 tablespoons chopped chutney) |
| Salt | |
| Melted butter or margarine | |

1. Sprinkle chicken with salt. Working with pieces skin side down, divide Apple-Raisin Stuffing among boned thighs, spooning it onto center of

each. Fold sides over stuffing and fasten with a small skewer.

2. Place chicken seam side down in a greased shallow baking dish and brush with the melted butter.

3. Bake at 400°F 20 minutes. Turn thighs and continue baking for 20 minutes, or until tender.

4. Serve with fluffy *whipped potatoes* and *chicken gravy*, canned or prepared from a mix.      6 SERVINGS

**APPLE-RAISIN STUFFING:** Mix ¾ *cup chopped pared apple, ¼ cup dark seedless raisins, 1 tablespoon finely chopped onion, and 2 tablespoons snipped parsley.*

*\*To bone chicken thighs:* Make a lengthwise cut through to bone along thinner side of thigh. Scrape flesh away from bone; remove and discard bone. Cut off the piece of cartilage. Spread out pieces, skin side down.

## HALIBURTON PHEASANT

*Pheasants are rather dry birds, but the bacon and frequent basting keep them moist.*

| | |
|---|---|
| 1 pheasant | 1 cup chopped celery |
| 1 teaspoon lemon juice | Melted butter |
| | 4 slices bacon |
| Salt and pepper | 1 cup boiling water |
| 1 cup chopped onion | ½ cup white wine |

1. Brush cavity of pheasant with lemon juice. Sprinkle with salt and pepper. Add onion and celery. Brush bird with melted butter and arrange bacon slices over top.

2. Put bird in roasting pan and add boiling water and wine. Cover pan.

3. Roast at 350°F 25 minutes per pound, basting every 15 minutes. Remove cover and bacon for last 20 minutes. If desired, thicken pan liquid with flour or cornstarch to make a thin gravy.

2 TO 4 SERVINGS

## PARRY SOUND SMELTS BAKED WITH WINE

| | |
|---|---|
| 8 or 10 smelts | ½ cup white wine |
| ½ cup chopped celery | ½ cup fine bread crumbs |
| ¼ cup finely grated carrot | |
| | Salt to taste |
| 1 teaspoon dried parsley flakes | ¼ teaspoon pepper |
| | 7 tablespoons butter |

1. Clean smelts and remove heads and tails.

2. Sprinkle celery, carrot, and parsley flakes in a greased baking dish. Lay smelts on top. Add wine, then bread crumbs, salt, and pepper. Dot with butter.

3. Bake at 475°F about 12 minutes, basting several times with the liquid in the pan.      4 OR 5 SERVINGS

## GRILLED ARCTIC CHAR

*Arctic char can be cooked in any of the conventional ways, but this method of marinating and grilling over charcoal or in the oven seems to bring out the best in it.*

| | |
|---|---|
| 1 Arctic char (about 3 to 4 lbs.), filleted | 2 cloves garlic, minced, or ½ teaspoon garlic powder |
| 1 cup oil | |
| ¼ cup vinegar | |
| 1 teaspoon thyme | Salt and pepper |

1. Put fish fillets into a shallow dish.

2. Mix oil, vinegar, thyme, and garlic; pour over fish. Marinate fillets 2 to 4 hours.

3. Drain off marinade and reserve. Sprinkle fish with salt and pepper.

4. Grill 10 minutes per inch thickness of fish, turn once and brush with marinade.

ABOUT 6 SERVINGS

## SALMON FLORENTINE

| | |
|---|---|
| 1 can (16 oz.) salmon, drained (reserve liquid) and flaked | 2 tablespoons finely chopped onion |
| | 1 pkg. (12 oz.) frozen chopped spinach, cooked and thoroughly drained |
| Milk | |
| 3 tablespoons butter or margarine | |
| 3 tablespoons flour | ⅛ teaspoon pepper |
| ½ teaspoon salt | Pinch ground nutmeg |
| ½ teaspoon dry mustard | ½ cup shredded sharp Cheddar cheese |
| ¼ teaspoon Tabasco | Paprika |
| 1 tablespoon butter or margarine | |

1. Add enough milk to salmon liquid to measure 1½ cups liquid.

2. Heat 3 tablespoons butter in a saucepan. Stir in flour, salt, and dry mustard. Heat until bubbly. Add the liquid gradually, stirring until blended. Bring to boiling; boil 1 to 2 minutes, stirring con-

stantly. Blend in Tabasco. Lightly mix in the flaked salmon. Keep mixture warm.

3. Meanwhile, heat 1 tablespoon butter in a skillet. Add onion and cook until soft. Mix with drained spinach, pepper, and nutmeg. Turn seasoned spinach into a greased shallow 1-quart baking dish. Spread the salmon mixture evenly over the spinach. Sprinkle with cheese and then paprika.

4. Heat in a 425°F oven about 8 minutes, or until cheese is melted. ABOUT 4 SERVINGS

## SPAGHETTI TURNOVER

| | |
|---|---|
| 8 oz. spaghetti, cooked | ¼ teaspoon pepper |
| ½ cup chopped celery | ½ cup evaporated milk |
| ¼ cup chopped onion | ¼ cup butter or |
| 1 tablespoon poppy seed | margarine |
| ½ teaspoon salt | 2 cups shredded sharp |
| | Cheddar cheese (8 oz.) |

1. Combine spaghetti, celery, onion, poppy seed, salt, pepper, and evaporated milk in a bowl.

2. Heat butter in a large skillet. Spoon half of spaghetti mixture into skillet; sprinkle with 1½ cups cheese. Top with remaining spaghetti mixture and cheese. Cover and cook over medium heat 25 to 30 minutes, running spatula under mixture occasionally to prevent sticking.

3. Unmold turnover on a serving platter. Garnish with *parsley*, if desired. ABOUT 6 SERVINGS

## GOLDEN HORSESHOE MACARONI MOUSSE

| | |
|---|---|
| 2 eggs, well beaten | 1 tablespoon chopped |
| 1½ teaspoons salt | onion |
| ¼ cup melted butter | ½ cup shredded |
| 1½ cups scalded milk | Cheddar cheese |
| 1 cup elbow macaroni, cooked | 1 cup soft bread crumbs |
| | 1 pkg. frozen mixed |
| 1 green pepper, finely chopped | vegetables |
| | Salt and pepper |
| 1 pimiento, finely chopped | Butter |

1. Combine all ingredients, except ½ cup of bread crumbs, frozen vegetables, salt, pepper, and remaining butter. Pack mixture into a greased ring mold. Sprinkle crumbs on top. Set mold in a pan of hot water.

2. Bake at 350°F 40 minutes.

3. Cook mixed vegetables according to directions on package; drain and toss with salt, pepper, and butter to taste.

4. Unmold macaroni ring, put vegetables in the center, and serve. ABOUT 4 SERVINGS

## HOLLAND MARSH CELERY LOAF

| | |
|---|---|
| 1 egg | 1 cup chopped celery |
| 1 tablespoon butter, melted | ½ onion, chopped |
| | ½ cup walnuts, chopped |
| ¾ cup tomato juice | |
| 1 slice bread, crumbled | ⅓ cup grated cheese |

1. Oil a 7x4x2-inch loaf pan. Mix ingredients well. Turn into pan and pack lightly.

2. Bake at 350°F 45 minutes. 3 OR 4 SERVINGS

## KITCHENER RUTABAGA SCALLOP

| | |
|---|---|
| 2 cups cooked rutabaga (yellow turnip) slices | ½ cup brown sugar |
| | 1 teaspoon salt |
| | 4 tablespoons butter |
| 1½ cups tart apple slices | 2 tablespoons water |

1. Arrange half of the rutabaga slices in a greased 1-quart casserole. Add half of apple slices, brown sugar, and salt; dot with half of butter. Repeat and add water. Cover casserole.

2. Bake at 350°F 30 minutes. 4 TO 6 SERVINGS

## RUTABAGA SUPREME

| | |
|---|---|
| 2½ lbs. rutabaga (yellow turnip), pared and cut in cubes or slices | ½ teaspoon pepper |
| | 1 tablespoon cracker crumbs |
| | 2 tablespoons grated |
| 2 tablespoons butter | Romano or Parmesan |
| 1 tablespoon cream | cheese |
| 2 teaspoons salt | 2 teaspoons butter |

1. Cook rutabaga in a small amount of boiling salted water until tender (15 to 20 minutes); drain well.

2. Rice or thoroughly mash rutabaga. Add 2

tablespoons butter, cream, salt, and pepper; whip until fluffy. Turn rutabaga into a greased 1-quart casserole. Mix cracker crumbs and cheese; sprinkle over rutabaga. Dot top with 2 teaspoons butter.
3. Bake at 325°F 15 to 20 minutes, or until lightly browned. 4 OR 5 SERVINGS

## CREAMY STUFFED TOMATOES

| | |
|---|---|
| 4 large firm ripe tomatoes, cut in halves | 2 egg yolks, slightly beaten |
| 2 cups shredded Swiss cheese | 1 cup cream |
| | ½ teaspoon salt |
| ½ cup chopped ripe olives | ⅛ teaspoon curry powder or ¼ teaspoon dry mustard |
| 2 tablespoons chopped parsley | 6 tablespoons coarse soft bread crumbs |
| 1 teaspoon instant minced onion | 2 tablespoons melted butter or margarine |

1. Scoop out seedy centers from tomato halves. Invert to drain.
2. Put cheese, olives, parsley, and onion into a bowl. Add a mixture of egg yolks, cream, salt, and curry powder or dry mustard.
3. Set tomato shells in a shallow baking dish. Sprinkle insides lightly with *salt*. Spoon in filling. Top with a mixture of crumbs and butter.
4. Bake at 350°F about 35 minutes. 4 SERVINGS

## FRESH SPINACH SOUFFLÉ

| | |
|---|---|
| 2 cups firmly packed finely chopped spinach | 3 tablespoons butter or margarine |
| ¼ cup finely chopped onion | ¼ cup flour |
| | 1 cup milk |
| 1 teaspoon salt | 3 egg yolks, well beaten |
| ½ teaspoon rosemary, crushed | 4 egg whites |
| | 2 teaspoons shredded Parmesan cheese |

1. Toss spinach, onion, salt, and rosemary together.
2. Heat butter in a saucepan; blend in flour. Heat until bubbly. Stir in the milk and bring to boiling; cook 1 minute, or until sauce thickens. Remove from heat.
3. Mix seasoned spinach with sauce; stir in beaten egg yolks; cool.

4. Meanwhile, beat egg whites until stiff, not dry, peaks are formed. Fold small amount of spinach mixture into egg whites, then quickly fold egg whites into remaining spinach mixture.
5. Turn into an ungreased 2-quart soufflé dish (straight-sided casserole). Sprinkle top with Parmesan cheese.
6. Bake at 350°F 40 minutes, or until soufflé is lightly browned. 6 SERVINGS

**SPINACH-BACON SOUFFLÉ:** Follow recipe for Fresh Spinach Soufflé. Substitute ¼ *cup chopped green onion (with tops)* for the onion. Omit salt with spinach. Mix in ½ *pound sliced bacon*, diced, fried, and drained. Omit rosemary; mix ¼ *to ½ teaspoon thyme* and ½ *teaspoon salt* with the flour.

## CONCORD GRAPE PIE

| | |
|---|---|
| 1 lb. Concord grapes | 2 egg whites |
| ¾ cup sugar | Few grains salt |
| 2 tablespoons flour | ¼ cup sugar |
| Few grains salt | ½ teaspoon vanilla extract |
| 2 egg yolks | |
| 1 tablespoon butter | 1 baked 9-in. pie shell |

1. Wash grapes; remove stems, then slip the skins. Put pulp into a saucepan and cook gently until seeds are loosened; rub pulp through colander.
2. Mix sugar, flour, and salt; add to grape pulp in saucepan. Mix in grape skins. Bring to boiling and cook 2 minutes, stirring constantly.
3. Beat egg yolks slightly and stir in a small amount of hot mixture; return to mixture in saucepan. Cook 2 minutes over medium heat, stirring constantly.
4. Remove from heat and mix in butter. Cool.
5. Beat egg whites and salt until frothy. Add sugar gradually, beating until stiff peaks are formed. Beat in vanilla extract.
6. Turn filling into baked pie shell. Pile meringue onto filling and swirl meringue, sealing to edge of crust.
7. Bake at 350°F about 15 minutes, or until meringue is lightly browned. ONE 9-INCH PIE

## OTTAWA VALLEY PUMPKIN PIE

1½ cups cooked or canned pumpkin
½ cup sugar
½ cup brown sugar
½ teaspoon *each* salt, ground cinnamon, ginger, and nutmeg
1 tablespoon molasses
2 eggs, slightly beaten
1 cup scalded milk
1 baked 9-in. pie shell

1. Combine all ingredients, except baked pie shell, in the top of a double boiler. Cook over boiling water until mixture is thick, stirring occasionally. Cool slightly.
2. Pour filling into pie shell. Serve warm or cold topped with *whipped cream*.          ONE 9-INCH PIE

## NIAGARA APPLE-CHEESE BETTY

3 cups coarse bread crumbs
1½ cups shredded sharp cheese
¾ cup sugar
1 teaspoon ground cinnamon
6 apples, pared, cored, and sliced
¼ cup cold water

1. Combine bread crumbs and cheese. Mix sugar and cinnamon. Arrange layers of apples, sugar mixture, and crumb mixture in a greased casserole, making 3 layers of each. Drizzle water over last sugar mixture and top with last crumb mixture.
2. Bake at 375°F about 45 minutes. Serve plain or with *cream*.          6 TO 8 SERVINGS

## OLD-FASHIONED RICE PUDDING

⅔ cup uncooked long grain rice
3 cups milk
¼ teaspoon salt
½ cup sugar
1 teaspoon vanilla extract
¼ teaspoon ground cinnamon
⅛ teaspoon ground nutmeg
½ cup heavy cream
1 can (19 oz.) peach slices, drained

1. Combine rice, milk, and salt in top of a double boiler. Cover and cook over simmering water, stirring occasionally, until rice is tender, about 1 hour. Remove from heat; add sugar, vanilla extract, and spices. Cool, then chill.
2. Whip cream until soft peaks are formed; fold into chilled rice mixture.
3. Arrange a few peach slices in sherbet glasses and top with rice pudding. Garnish with peach slices, if desired.          6 TO 8 SERVINGS

## PEACH PUFFS

3 tablespoons butter
4 eggs
1 cup milk
Thin outer peel of ½ lemon
1 cup sifted all-purpose flour
2 tablespoons sugar
½ teaspoon salt
1½ cups heavy cream
3 tablespoons confectioners' sugar
¼ teaspoon ground cinnamon
⅛ teaspoon ground nutmeg
4 cups fresh, canned, or thawed frozen peach slices

1. Put 1½ tablespoons butter into each of two 9-inch pie pans. Set in oven while oven is preheating.
2. Put eggs, milk, and lemon peel into an electric blender container. Cover and blend at high speed until thoroughly combined and lemon peel is finely chopped. Add flour, sugar, and salt. Blend at high speed until smooth; scrape down sides of blender container if necessary. Pour half of batter into each pie pan with melted butter.
3. Bake at 400°F 20 to 22 minutes, or until puffed and golden.
4. Whip cream until soft peaks are formed. Beat in confectioners' sugar and spices. Put half of peaches in center of each pancake. Sprinkle with *confectioners' sugar*. Cut into wedges and spoon whipped cream over individual servings.

10 TO 12 SERVINGS

## CLOVER-ROSE HONEY: OR HOW TO MAKE HONEY WITHOUT BEES

2 cups boiling water
4 cups sugar
Pinch of alum
20 pink clover heads
20 white clover heads
Head of 1 rose

1. Combine boiling water and sugar; bring to boiling, reduce heat, and simmer until syrup begins to thicken. Stir in alum; boil 3 minutes. Add clover and rose; boil 3 minutes. Strain.
2. Pour into sterilized jars; seal.

# QUEBEC

QUEBEC ☐

French-Canadian cuisine is unique in Canada, based as it is on the culinary arts of France, brought to Canada more than 300 years ago. Many recipes date back to 1646 when the Ursuline Sisters of Quebec adapted Norman dishes to local ingredients. Even today, four out of five of the inhabitants of Quebec claim France as their country of origin, and the best cooking in the province is still based on dishes which have been handed down through a dozen generations.

Pork is an important item on the shopping list, and there are many delightful ways of serving it. The thrifty settlers used every bit they could, and some delicious dishes are made of pigs' feet, cheeks, and even tails! Tourtière is a pork pie with a golden crust, served traditionally on Christmas Eve after midnight mass. Salt fat pork turns up in many recipes. In Quebec, this little pig really goes to market!

Maple groves are abundant, and from the thin sap collected in late winter, come the sweet, uniquely flavored maple sugar and maple syrup used in unlikely but delicious combinations.

Pea soup and onion soup, made by the methods given here, are traditionally French-Canadian.

Wild game abounds in Quebec, and the method of boiling partridge in cabbage, with, of course, the inevitable bits of salt pork, brings out the best in flavor. Brome Lake ducklings were found wild in the Eastern Townships but have been domesticated and have a very special taste.

There are various cheeses made in Quebec which are quite unique, partly due to the fact that some of them are made in monasteries, and the processes used are not divulged. One not made by farming monks is Fromage di l'Île, a pungent cheese from L'Île d'Orléans, where it is said only ten families know the secret of making it.

🍁43

## CHEESE PÂTÉ PUFFS

*These unusually flavored, flaky morsels resembling miniature pasties can be prepared ahead of time, refrigerated, and popped into the oven a few minutes before serving.*

| | |
|---|---|
| 1 cup all-purpose flour | 2 teaspoons finely |
| 2 tablespoons toasted | chopped onion |
| sesame seed | 1 can (2¼ oz.) liver |
| ½ cup butter | pâté |
| 3 oz. sharp Cheddar | |
| cheese, cut in small | |
| pieces (about ¾ cup) | |

1. Combine flour with sesame seed in a bowl. Using a pastry blender or two knives, cut in the butter and cheese.
2. Shape into a ball, wrap in waxed paper, and refrigerate 6 hours, or until thoroughly chilled.
3. Remove pastry about 15 minutes before it is to be used, then roll ⅛ inch thick on lightly floured surface. Cut into 2-inch rounds.
4. Stir chopped onion into liver pâté and spoon about ½ teaspoon of the mixture onto center of each round. Fold one half over other half and press edges gently; arrange 1 inch apart on baking sheet.
5. Bake at 450°F 8 to 10 minutes, or until puffs are golden brown. ABOUT 1½ DOZEN PUFFS

NOTE: *1 teaspoon dill weed* may be substituted for the sesame seed in the pastry.

## PÂTÉ DE FOIE GRAS

*Originally this delicious appetizer was made of goose liver, which nowadays is almost impossible to buy in the market.*

| | |
|---|---|
| 1 lb. chicken livers | 1 egg, slightly beaten |
| 2 to 3 tablespoons | 1½ teaspoons salt |
| minced onion | ¼ teaspoon pepper |
| 3 cloves garlic, | Pinch of marjoram |
| minced | Bay leaf, crushed |
| 1 slice bread, grated | Thyme, fresh or |
| ½ lb. butter, softened | powdered dry |

1. Chill livers, then mince them. Mix with onion, minced garlic from 2 cloves, and bread. Add butter, egg, salt, pepper, and marjoram; beat very well.
2. Turn mixture into a baking dish. Top with minced garlic from 1 clove, pieces of bay leaf, and thyme. Put the dish in a deep pan and fill pan with hot water to level of meat.

3. Bake at 300°F about 1 hour per pound. Let it cool in the pan of water.
4. Serve cold on *toast rounds* or *crackers*, or sliced with hors d'oeuvres. ABOUT 3 CUPS PÂTÉ

## FRENCH-CANADIAN ONION SOUP

| | |
|---|---|
| 3 large onions, thinly | Few drops Tabasco |
| sliced | Salt and pepper |
| ½ cup butter or | to taste |
| vegetable oil | 6 slices toast |
| 1½ tablespoons flour | 4 oz. grated Cheddar |
| 5½ cups seasoned | cheese |
| meat stock | |

1. Fry onions in oil until golden brown. Stir in flour, then stock and seasonings; simmer 10 minutes.
2. Pour soup into individual ovenproof dishes, put a slice of toast on top, and cover with cheese. Broil 3 to 4 minutes until cheese is melted and bubbly. 6 SERVINGS

## HABITANT PEA SOUP

| | |
|---|---|
| 2 cups dried whole | 1 tablespoon chopped |
| yellow peas | parsley, ½ teaspoon |
| 2 qts. water | sage, *or* 1 teaspoon |
| 1 onion, minced | salted herbs |
| ¼ to ½ lb. salt pork | Salt and pepper to taste |

1. Soak peas in cold water overnight.
2. The next day, add onion, salt pork, and desired seasoning. Cover, bring to boiling, reduce heat, and simmer 3 to 4 hours. Mix in salt and pepper. ABOUT 8 SERVINGS

NOTE: If pork is too salty, boil it for 5 minutes and drain before adding to the soup.

## ROASTED PIGS' TAILS

Clean, singe and wash the *pigs' tails.* Simmer them for about an hour in *salted water* to which has been added a *carrot,* an *onion pierced with a clove,* and a *bouquet garni,* consisting of *2 stalks celery, 2 sprigs parsley, ½ bay leaf, 3 peppercorns, 1 clove* and *¼ teaspoon thyme,* tied in a cheesecloth bag. Arrange them flat in a platter, pour the liquid over, and let cool. Drain them well; roll them in *melted butter or shortening*, then in *bread crumbs*, and roast them in a slow oven. Serve hot as an hors d'oeuvre or as an entrée, if you have enough.

NOTE: Usually you have to give your butcher several weeks' notice so that he can save them up for you.

## TOURTIÈRE

*This is a tasty pork pie, traditionally eaten at Christmastime, particularly on Christmas Eve after the midnight mass. These are the basic ingredients, but it is difficult to find two Quebec housewives who make it the same way. A frequent variation is the addition of a minced garlic clove, celery salt, or cooked mashed potato.*

| | |
|---|---|
| 1½ lbs. ground lean pork | ½ teaspoon sage |
| 1 small onion, chopped | ¼ cup water |
| 1 teaspoon salt | Pastry for a 2-crust 9-in. pie |

1. Combine pork, onion, salt, sage, and water in a saucepan. Bring to boiling, reduce heat, and cook 25 minutes. Cool.
2. Prepare pastry. Turn pork mixture into unbaked pie shell. Cover with top crust.
3. Bake at 450°F 15 minutes, then reduce oven temperature to 350°F and bake 5 to 10 minutes, or until pastry is browned. ABOUT 6 SERVINGS

## CRETONS

*This is a very tasty meat treat, usually sliced and served cold between slices of French or rye bread.*

| | |
|---|---|
| 1½ lbs. leaf lard, cut in small pieces | ½ teaspoon pepper |
| 3 lbs. lean pork, cut in pieces | 1 teaspoon ground cloves |
| 3 large onions, cut in pieces | 1 teaspoon ground allspice |
| 1 tablespoon salt | ½ cup dry bread crumbs |
| 1 tablespoon ground cinnamon | |

1. Heat leaf lard in a heavy saucepan; cook until the fat separates, leaving crisp cracklings. Drain.
2. Grind cracklings with pork and onions. Add seasonings and cook, stirring occasionally, until meat is well done. Stir in bread crumbs.
3. Put mixture into small molds which have been rinsed in cold water. Chill. ABOUT 6 CUPS PÂTÉ

## PORK LOIN ROAST

| | |
|---|---|
| 1 pork loin roast (4 to 6 lbs.) | Salt and pepper |
| | Spiced crab apples |

1. Have meat retailer saw across the rib bones of roast at base of the backbone, separating the ribs from the backbone. Place roast, fat side up, on a rack in an open roasting pan. Season with salt and pepper. Insert meat thermometer in roast so the bulb is centered in the thickest part and not resting on bone or in fat.
2. Roast in a 350°F oven about 2½ to 3 hours, or until thermometer registers 170°F; allow 30 to 40 minutes per pound.
3. For easy carving, remove backbone, place roast on platter, and allow roast to set for 15 to 20 minutes. Garnish platter with spiced crab apples, heated if desired.
4. Accompany with Hash Brown Potatoes au Gratin *(page 56)*. 8 TO 10 SERVINGS

## LAURENTIAN PORK CHOPS AND MAPLE SUGAR

| | |
|---|---|
| 6 pork chops, cut about 1 in. thick | 3 red apples, cored and halved |
| 1 teaspoon salt | 6 tablespoons grated maple sugar |
| ⅛ teaspoon pepper | 1 cup light cream |

1. Brown chops evenly on both sides in a skillet. Drain off fat if necessary. Season chops with salt and pepper.
2. Put apple halves, cut side up, on chops and top with maple sugar. Pour in cream and cover. Cook over low heat about 45 minutes, or until chops are tender. 6 SERVINGS

## PORK CHOPS AND LIMAS

| | |
|---|---|
| 4 pork chops, cut ¾ to 1 in. thick | ½ cup chopped onion |
| 1 teaspoon fat | 1 to 2 tablespoons dark molasses |
| 2¼ cups cooked lima beans | 2 teaspoons salt |
| 1 can (19 oz.) tomatoes, drained | ¼ teaspoon pepper |

1. Brown chops in fat in a skillet.
2. While chops are browning, turn lima beans

into a shallow 2-qt. casserole or baking dish. Sieve tomatoes and add to the casserole along with onion, molasses, and 1 teaspoon salt.

3. Season chops with remaining salt and the pepper. Arrange chops over lima bean mixture.

4. Bake at 350°F 1 hour, or until meat is tender.

4 SERVINGS

## BAKED PORK CHOPS WITH JELLY GLAZE

¼ cup all-purpose flour
2 teaspoons salt
¼ teaspoon pepper
1 teaspoon fat
6 pork loin chops, cut about 1 in. thick
⅔ cup hot water
3 tablespoons minced onion

2 tablespoons minced parsley
½ cup currant jelly, broken in pieces with a fork
¼ cup hot water
¼ teaspoon ground cinnamon
¼ teaspoon ground cloves

1. Mix flour, salt, and pepper. Coat pork chops evenly.

2. Heat fat in a large heavy skillet. Add chops and brown lightly on both sides. Place browned chops in a large shallow baking dish. Add ⅔ cup hot water, onion, and parsley. Cover tightly with baking dish cover or aluminum foil.

3. Bake at 350°F about 45 minutes.

4. Meanwhile, combine jelly, ¼ cup hot water, cinnamon, and cloves in a heavy saucepan. Set over low heat, stirring occasionally, until jelly is melted.

5. Uncover baking dish and pour jelly glaze over the chops. Continue baking 20 minutes, or until chops are tender.

6 SERVINGS

## OVEN-ROASTED SAUCED SPARERIBS

2 sides pork spareribs (3 to 3½ lbs.)
¼ cup firmly packed brown sugar
2 teaspoons dry mustard
¼ teaspoon pepper
1 cup ketchup
½ cup cider vinegar

½ cup water
3 tablespoons Worcestershire sauce
2 tablespoons grated onion
1 clove garlic, crushed in garlic press

1. Leave spareribs whole or cut into serving-sized pieces. Place in a large shallow pan. Roast at 350°F 30 minutes.

2. Combine brown sugar, dry mustard, and pepper in a saucepan and blend thoroughly. Stir in remaining ingredients and bring to boiling over medium heat, stirring occasionally.

3. Pour half of the sauce over ribs and continue roasting 30 minutes.

4. Turn ribs and pour on remaining sauce. Roast 30 to 45 minutes, or until meat is tender.

4 OR 5 SERVINGS

## VEAL SUPREME

1 lb. thin veal scallops or cutlets, flattened
3 tablespoons lemon juice
5 tablespoons butter

2 cups sliced fresh mushrooms
1 cup light cream
1 tablespoon flour
½ teaspoon salt

1. Cut veal into serving-sized pieces. Put into a shallow dish and drizzle with lemon juice. Cover and refrigerate 2 hours. Drain veal and pat dry with paper towels.

2. Heat a large skillet; melt 3 tablespoons butter. Add veal and cook until lightly browned on both sides. Remove to a heated platter and keep warm.

3. Add remaining 2 tablespoons butter to skillet. Add mushrooms and sauté until tender.

4. Combine cream, flour, and salt; pour into skillet. Bring to boiling, stirring constantly; cook 1 minute.

5. Pour mushroom sauce around veal. Garnish with *parsley*. Serve immediately. ABOUT 4 SERVINGS

## CHEESE-FILLED VEAL ROLLS

1 lb. ground veal
¼ cup finely chopped onion
¾ teaspoon salt
⅛ teaspoon pepper
Few grains cayenne pepper

4 slices (4 oz.) process American cheese, cut lengthwise in quarters
2 tablespoons butter or margarine

1. Lightly toss together ground veal, onion, salt, and peppers. Divide into 8 equal portions. Shape each into a rectangle about 4 inches long and ¼ inch thick. Stack two strips of cheese and place on the center of a rectangle of meat. Fold meat around cheese to form a roll, enclosing it completely. Repeat for remaining portions of meat.

2. Brown meat on both sides in hot butter in a

large heavy skillet, allowing about 25 minutes for cooking.

3. Serve with hot fluffy *rice* and a garnish of any heated *canned or cooked fruit*.   ABOUT 4 SERVINGS

## BROME LAKE DUCKLING WITH SAGE AND ONION STUFFING

*These succulent ducklings are grown near Brome Lake in the Eastern Townships of Quebec and are exported in large quantities.*

| | |
|---|---|
| 1½ cups chopped onion | 2 teaspoons crushed |
| ¼ cup butter | fresh sage or |
| 1 finely chopped duck | powdered sage |
| or goose liver | ½ teaspoon salt |
| (optional) | ¼ teaspoon pepper |
| 1 beaten egg | 1 duckling |
| 4 cups soft, stale | Orange Glaze, *below* |
| bread crumbs | |

1. Sauté onion in butter, then add chopped liver and cook about 1 minute.
2. Mix egg, bread crumbs, and seasonings. Add onion and liver; toss to mix. Stuff duckling lightly; prick the skin thoroughly.
3. Put the duckling, breast down, on a rack in a shallow roasting pan.
4. Roast at 350°F 45 minutes. Turn duckling breast up; prick the skin and pour off the fat as it accumulates. Roast about 1¼ hours longer.
5. Remove duckling from pan and keep it warm. Drain off all the fat in the pan. Add Orange Glaze to drippings and cook-stir about 5 minutes. Return duckling to pan and baste with glaze. Continue roasting about 30 minutes, basting several times.

ABOUT 4 SERVINGS

### ORANGE GLAZE

| | |
|---|---|
| 1 orange | 2 tablespoons lemon |
| ½ cup water | juice |
| 2 tablespoons jelly | ½ cup giblet stock |
| | or bouillon |

Grate the orange peel and combine with water; simmer 10 minutes, then drain. Cut up orange pulp and mix with orange peel, jelly, lemon juice, and stock.

## DUCKLING DE POMME

| | |
|---|---|
| 2 ducklings (4 lbs. | ½ cup sliced green |
| each), quartered | onion (with tops) |
| 1½ teaspoons salt | ¼ cup snipped parsley |
| ½ teaspoon pepper | 1 teaspoon thyme |
| 2 tablespoons butter | ½ cup apple cider |
| or margarine | 2 tablespoons flour |
| ¾ cup applejack | 1 cup light cream |

1. Rinse duckling pieces (omit wings, necks, and backs) and drain on absorbent paper. Using kitchen shears or a knife, cut off excess fat. Rub duckling with a mixture of the salt and pepper.
2. Heat butter in a large skillet; add duckling. Sauté until well browned on all sides. Remove to absorbent paper.
3. Pour off drippings and return duckling to hot skillet. Pour applejack over duckling and ignite. When flame dies down, add sliced onion, parsley, thyme, and apple cider.
4. Cover skillet tightly and simmer slowly until duckling is tender. Transfer to heated platter and keep warm.
5. Stir flour into liquid in skillet and cook, stirring constantly, until bubbly. Blend in cream; cook until sauce is thickened and smooth, stirring constantly.
6. Pour sauce over duckling. Garnish platter with *watercress* and *spiced crab apples*.

ABOUT 6 SERVINGS

## PERDRIX AUX CHAUX

*If you should be fortunate enough to get some partridge, here is a lovely thing to do with it.*

| | |
|---|---|
| 2 or 3 partridge | 1 carrot |
| 3 small strips salt | 1 onion |
| pork | 3 cloves |
| 2 or 3 small cabbages | Salt and pepper |

1. Sear partridge along with strips of salt pork.
2. Dip cabbage in boiling water for 1 minute, then remove core and pull the leaves apart. Drain well. Place a layer of cabbage leaves in the bottom of a small roasting pan. Set partridge on cabbage together with crisped pork; cover with cabbage leaves. Or wrap the partridge individually in cabbage leaves. Add carrot and onion with cloves stuck in it. Sprinkle with salt and pepper. Cover with 1 inch of *boiling water*. Cover pan.
3. Cook at 350°F 1 to 1½ hours.   4 TO 6 SERVINGS

## TOMATOES VINAIGRETTE

4 medium tomatoes, sliced
2 medium cucumbers, thinly sliced
1 medium onion, sliced
1 cup salad oil
½ cup wine vinegar
1 teaspoon salt
¼ teaspoon pepper
½ teaspoon savory
½ teaspoon tarragon
½ teaspoon crumbled bay leaf
½ teaspoon celery salt

1. Alternate layers of tomato, cucumber, and onion rings in a shallow dish.
2. Combine the remaining ingredients. Pour over vegetables, cover, and refrigerate 12 hours.
3. Spoon vegetables onto *shredded lettuce* and sprinkle with *snipped parsley*.     12 SERVINGS

## BRANDY ALEXANDER PIE

1⅓ cups chocolate wafer crumbs
3 tablespoons butter, melted
1 env. unflavored gelatin
¾ cup sugar
¼ teaspoon salt
3 egg yolks
⅔ cup milk
⅓ cup crème de cacao
2 tablespoons brandy
3 egg whites
1 cup heavy cream

1. Mix wafer crumbs and butter. Turn into a 9-inch pie pan and press firmly onto bottom and sides. Chill.
2. Mix gelatin, ½ cup sugar, and salt in a saucepan. Beat egg yolks and milk together; add gradually to gelatin mixture, stirring constantly. Cook over low heat, stirring constantly, until gelatin and sugar are dissolved.
3. Remove from heat. Stir in crème de cacao and brandy. Chill until slightly thickened.
4. Beat egg whites until frothy. Add ¼ cup sugar gradually, beating until stiff peaks are formed. Whip cream until peaks are formed. Fold meringue and whipped cream into gelatin mixture. Chill until mixture will mound.
5. Pile filling into pie shell. Chill until firm. If desired, garnish with *chocolate curls*.   ONE 9-INCH PIE

## EASTERN TOWNSHIPS MAPLE SYRUP PIE

Pastry for a 2-crust 9-in. pie
1 cup maple syrup
½ cup boiling water
3 tablespoons cornstarch
3 tablespoons cold water
1 tablespoon butter
Chopped nuts

1. Prepare pastry.
2. Combine maple syrup and water; boil 5 minutes. Mix cornstarch and cold water; stir into boiling mixture. Bring again to boiling and stir until thickened. Add butter; stir until melted. Pour into pie shell. Sprinkle nuts over top. Cover with top pastry.
3. Bake at 400°F 30 minutes, or until top is golden brown.     ONE 9-INCH PIE

## CORNSTARCH BLANCMANGE

⅓ cup sugar
3 tablespoons cornstarch
⅛ teaspoon salt
½ cup cold milk
1½ cups milk, heated
1 teaspoon vanilla extract
4 egg whites

1. Mix sugar, cornstarch, and salt in a saucepan. Stir in cold milk. Add hot milk gradually, stirring constantly. Bring to boiling, stirring constantly; cook 1 minute.
2. Remove from heat. Blend in vanilla extract.
3. Beat egg whites until rounded peaks are formed. Spread over cornstarch mixture and fold together. Turn into a 1-quart mold and chill until firm.
4. Unmold onto a chilled serving plate and serve with desired *fruit sauce*.     ABOUT 6 SERVINGS

## MONTREAL MELON AND OKA OR ERMITE CHEESE

Perhaps after some of these rather rich delicacies, you would like a simple dessert. A delicious and refreshing combination is Montreal Melon with either Oka or Ermite cheese. Montreal melon is a special variety of melon with exquisite flavor. Oka cheese is a local, rather strong cheese, for years made at a Trappist monastery near the town of Oka. Ermite is another local cheese, also made at a monastery at St. Benoit du Lac.

# NEW BRUNSWICK

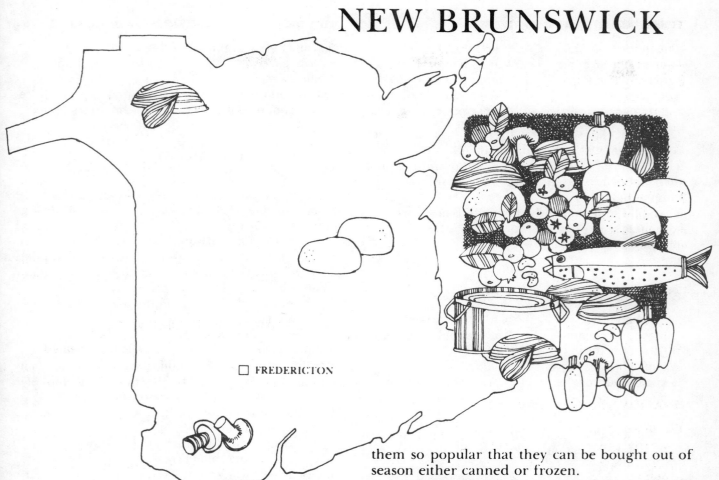

□ FREDERICTON

New Brunswick has several native delicacies, and the first that come to mind are its delicious varieties of seafood and the excellent potatoes for which the province is famous. There is a long-standing argument among gourmets as to the relative excellence of British Columbia and New Brunswick salmon: whichever is better will never be settled, and East Coast salmon is certainly delicious. So are Buctouche and Caraquet oysters and lobsters which come mainly from the Shediac area, once known as the lobster capital of the world. Clams are large and New Brunswickers have evolved a clam chowder that evokes nostalgic longing in anyone who has ever tasted it. A less known fish, shad, has a taste all its own.

Unique to the province are fiddleheads, an edible form of the ostrich fern which is picked in spring. Their delicate flavor, either as a hot buttered vegetable or cold in salads, has made them so popular that they can be bought out of season either canned or frozen.

Another native delicacy, not always so much appreciated by a tourist, is dulse. This is a type of seaweed resembling kelp which is harvested at low tide, dried, and eaten as a snack.

## CLAM DIP
*Try this dip with raw cauliflowerets as dippers.*

| | |
|---|---|
| 1 can (10½ oz.) clams | ½ teaspoon salt |
| 6 oz. cream cheese, cut in pieces | ¼ teaspoon freshly ground pepper |
| 1 tablespoon lemon juice | 4 drops Tabasco |
| 1 teaspoon Worcestershire sauce | Few sprigs parsley |

1. Drain clams, reserving ¼ cup liquid. Put liquid into an electric blender container with the remaining ingredients except clams. Cover and blend.
2. Add clams and blend well.     ABOUT 2 CUPS DIP
NOTE: *Canned minced clams* may be used if an electric blender is not available.

🍁 49

## SHEDIAC CLAM CHOWDER

| | |
|---|---|
| 1 qt. clams | 1½ cups boiling water |
| ½ lb. salt pork, diced | 1 qt. rich milk |
| 1 onion, diced | 1 teaspoon salt |
| 4 cups diced raw | ⅛ teaspoon pepper |
| potatoes | 1 tablespoon butter |

1.   Clean clams and cut them into small pieces. Brown them with salt pork and onion.
2.   Cook potatoes in boiling water until tender, then add clams, salt pork, and onion; simmer 2 minutes.
3.   Scald milk and add it to potatoes along with the seasonings.
4.   Just before serving, stir in butter.

8 TO 10 SERVINGS

## ST. JOHN RIVER SHAD AMANDINE

| | |
|---|---|
| 2 lbs. shad fillets | ¼ to ½ cup fat or oil |
| ½ teaspoon salt | 2 tablespoons lemon |
| ⅛ teaspoon pepper | juice |
| ½ cup milk | ½ cup almonds, |
| ½ cup all-purpose flour | blanched and slivered |
| ¾ cup dry bread | ½ cup butter |
| crumbs | |

1.   Season fillets with salt and pepper. Dip them in milk, then in flour, then in milk again, then in bread crumbs.
2.   Brown fish in hot fat, then cook 10 minutes per inch thickness of fish, turning once. Drain fish and arrange on heated platter. Drizzle with lemon juice.
3.   Heat the almonds in butter until golden brown. Pour almonds and butter over fish.

ABOUT 6 SERVINGS

## RESTIGOUCHE SALMON

| | |
|---|---|
| 2 lbs. salmon steaks | ½ teaspoon salt |
| 1 teaspoon grated lemon | ⅛ teaspoon pepper |
| peel | ¼ teaspoon marjoram |
| 3 tablespoons lemon | 1 tablespoon finely |
| juice | chopped onion |
| ¼ cup salad oil | |

1.   Put salmon steaks into a greased broiler pan. Combine lemon peel, lemon juice, oil, seasonings, and onion. Pour over salmon. Marinate 20 minutes, turning once.
2.   Broil 5 minutes on each side for 1-inch steaks.

4 TO 6 SERVINGS

## SALMON SOUFFLÉ WITH DILL SAUCE

| | |
|---|---|
| 2 salmon steaks, about | 1 cup milk |
| ⅓ lb. each | 2 teaspoons grated |
| Boiling water | onion |
| ½ teaspoon salt | 2 teaspoons lemon juice |
| 3 tablespoons butter or | 2 tablespoons snipped |
| margarine | parsley |
| 3 tablespoons flour | 3 egg yolks |
| ½ teaspoon salt | 3 egg whites |
| ½ teaspoon paprika | Dill Sauce, *below* |

1.   Put salmon steaks in a single layer on a large square of cheesecloth. Pull up corners of cheesecloth and tie together. Place in a saucepan and cover with boiling water; add ½ teaspoon salt. Bring water to boiling, reduce heat, and simmer, covered, about 15 minutes, or until salmon flakes easily when tested with a fork.
2.   Remove salmon from liquid and discard bones and skin; flake and set aside.
3.   Heat butter in a saucepan. Blend in flour, ½ teaspoon salt, and paprika. Cook, stirring constantly, until bubbly. Add milk gradually, continuing to stir. Bring rapidly to boiling and boil 1 to 2 minutes, stirring constantly.
4.   Remove from heat. Stir in onion, lemon juice, parsley, and salmon.
5.   Beat egg yolks until thick; add sauce, a small amount at a time, blending after each addition.
6.   Beat egg whites until stiff, not dry, peaks are formed. Add salmon sauce in thirds, gently folding until blended after each addition.
7.   Turn mixture into a lightly greased (bottom only) 1-quart soufflé dish.
8.   Bake at 325°F 50 to 60 minutes, or until a knife comes our clean when inserted halfway between center and edge of soufflé.
9.   Serve with Dill Sauce.

ABOUT 6 SERVINGS

## DILL SAUCE

| | |
|---|---|
| 2 tablespoons butter | Few grains pepper |
| or margarine | ½ teaspoon dill |
| ¼ cup chopped onion | weed, crushed |
| ¼ cup chopped | 1 cup milk |
| mushrooms | 1 teaspoon grated |
| 2 tablespoons flour | lemon peel |
| ¼ teaspoon salt | |

Heat butter in a heavy saucepan. Mix in onion and mushrooms and cook about 5 minutes. Blend in flour, salt, pepper, and dill. Cook, stirring constantly, until bubbly. Add milk gradually, continuing to stir. Mix in lemon peel. Bring to boiling and boil 1 to 2 minutes, stirring constantly. Serve hot over soufflé.

ABOUT 1 CUP SAUCE

## FIDDLEHEADS

These delicious little greens should be sparingly boiled in a little water, then buttered and seasoned. They are just fine by themselves, but they can be dressed up by the addition of a few slivered almonds or a white or Hollandaise sauce. Cold, they add an interesting note to salads.

## FUNDY BAKED BEANS

| | |
|---|---|
| 2 cups dried beans | Salt and pepper |
| 1½ qts. cold water | 1 teaspoon dry mustard |
| 1 teaspoon salt | ½ cup molasses or |
| 1 medium onion | ¼ cup molasses and |
| ¼ lb. salt pork, sliced | ⅓ cup brown sugar |

1. Rinse beans; cover with cold water and soak overnight.
2. Next morning, add 1 teaspoon salt to beans and soaking water; cover, simmer about 1 hour. Drain, reserving 3 cups bean liquid. Put the onion and salt pork into bean pot. Add beans, salt and pepper to taste, dry mustard, molasses, and reserved bean liquid to cover; mix well. Cover.
3. Bake at 300°F about 3 hours. Add liquid as needed. Remove cover for last 25 minutes.

ABOUT 6 SERVINGS

## CORN EN CASSEROLE

| | |
|---|---|
| 1½ cups ready-to-eat bran flakes | ¼ teaspoon paprika |
| ¼ cup chopped green pepper | ¼ teaspoon dry mustard |
| ¼ cup finely chopped onion | 1¼ cups milk |
| 2 tablespoons butter or margarine | 2 tablespoons diced pimiento |
| 2 tablespoons flour | 2 eggs, well beaten |
| 1 teaspoon sugar | 2 cans (10 oz. each) whole kernel corn, drained |
| 1 teaspoon salt | 1 tablespoon butter or margarine, melted |
| ⅛ teaspoon pepper | |

1. Crush ¾ cup of the cereal; set aside.
2. Cook green pepper and onion in 2 tablespoons hot butter in a saucepan about 5 minutes.

3. Blend in a mixture of flour, sugar, salt, pepper, paprika, and dry mustard. Heat until bubbly. Stir in the milk and bring to boiling; cook 1 to 2 minutes. Mix in pimiento.
4. Stir a small amount of hot sauce into beaten eggs. Immediately blend into sauce. Stir in crushed cereal and corn until blended. Turn into a greased 1½-quart casserole.
5. Toss the melted butter lightly with remaining ¾ cup cereal. Sprinkle evenly over corn mixture.
6. Bake at 375°F about 25 minutes.

6 TO 8 SERVINGS

## TANTRAMAR MUSHROOMS

| | |
|---|---|
| 1 lb. fresh mushrooms | 2 tablespoons flour |
| 1 tablespoon grated onion | 1 teaspoon salt |
| ½ clove garlic, minced | ¼ teaspoon pepper |
| 3 tablespoons butter | 1 teaspoon celery seed |
| 2 teaspoons lemon juice | 1 cup chicken stock |
| | ½ cup light cream |
| | Hot buttered toast |

1. Clean and slice mushrooms.
2. Sauté onion and garlic in butter 2 minutes. Add mushrooms and lemon juice; simmer until mushrooms are tender, about 3 minutes. Sprinkle with flour, salt, pepper, and celery seed; stir to blend. Add chicken stock and cream; bring to boiling and cook-stir until thick and smooth.
3. Serve immediately over toast.

ABOUT 6 SERVINGS

## BAKED POTATOES À LA MOFFAT

| | |
|---|---|
| 5 medium-sized baking potatoes, baked | 1 cup chopped onion |
| 3 tablespoons butter or margarine | 2 tablespoons snipped parsley |
| 1 teaspoon salt | 6 slices sharp process Cheddar cheese, each cut in 6 strips |
| ⅛ teaspoon white pepper | |
| ½ cup hot milk or cream | |

1. Halve the baked potatoes lengthwise. With a spoon, scoop out insides without breaking skins.
2. Mash or rice potatoes. Add butter, salt, and pepper. Gradually add hot milk, whipping until potatoes are fluffy. Beat in onion and parsley until thoroughly combined.
3. Pile mixture lightly into potato skins, leaving surfaces uneven. Top each potato half with 3 cheese strips. Sprinkle with *paprika*.

4. Place potato halves under broiler with tops about 3 inches from source of heat. Broil about 1 minute, or until cheese melts.

*10 FILLED POTATO HALVES*

## GREEN BEANS WITH TOMATO

¼ cup finely chopped onion
1 small clove garlic, minced
¼ cup butter or margarine
1 tablespoon lemon juice
2 medium ripe tomatoes, cut in pieces
1 tablespoon brown sugar
1 teaspoon salt
⅛ teaspoon pepper
½ teaspoon oregano
1 lb. fresh green beans, cut diagonally in 1-in. pieces, cooked, and drained

1. Cook onion and garlic in butter in a skillet 3 minutes. Add remaining ingredients except beans and heat thoroughly.
2. Toss tomato mixture and hot beans together. Serve immediately. *6 TO 8 SERVINGS*

## GOURMET POTATO SALAD

5 cups cubed cooked potatoes
½ teaspoon salt
⅛ teaspoon pepper
4 hard-cooked eggs, chopped
1 cup chopped celery
⅔ cup sliced green onions
¼ cup chopped green pepper
1 cup large-curd creamed cottage cheese
¼ teaspoon dry mustard
½ teaspoon salt
Few grains pepper
⅔ cup undiluted evaporated milk
½ cup crumbled blue cheese
2 tablespoons cider vinegar

1. Put potatoes into a large mixing bowl and season with a mixture of the salt and pepper. Add eggs, celery, green onions, and green pepper; toss lightly.
2. Combine cottage cheese with remaining ingredients in an electric blender container and blend thoroughly.
3. Pour dressing over mixture in bowl and toss lightly and thoroughly. Chill before serving to blend flavors. Turn into a bowl lined with *lettuce* and garnish with a sliced *hard-cooked egg* and additional blue cheese. *ABOUT 8 SERVINGS*

## BUTTERSCOTCH CREAM PIE OR TARTS

1 cup firmly packed dark brown sugar
¼ cup flour
¼ teaspoon salt
½ cup milk
1½ cups milk, scalded
3 egg yolks, slightly beaten
3 tablespoons butter
2 teaspoons vanilla extract
1 baked 8-inch pie shell or 6 baked 3½-inch tart shells

1. Combine the brown sugar, flour, and salt in the top of a double boiler. Blend in ½ cup milk; mix thoroughly. Gradually add the scalded milk, stirring until blended. Bring rapidly to boiling and cook 3 minutes. Set over boiling water; cover and cook 5 to 7 minutes, stirring 3 or 4 times.
2. Stir about 3 tablespoons of hot mixture into slightly beaten egg yolks. Immediately blend into mixture in double boiler. Cook and stir over boiling water 3 to 5 minutes.
3. Remove from water and blend in the butter and vanilla extract. Cool slightly, stirring occasionally. Cover; cool to lukewarm in refrigerator.
4. Turn filling into pie shell or tart shells. Chill, if desired.
5. Top pie or tarts with *sweetened whipped cream* and *toasted almonds or pecans*.

*ONE 8-INCH PIE OR SIX 3½-INCH TARTS*

## CHARLOTTE COUNTY BLUEBERRY CRISP

4 cups blueberries
2 teaspoons lemon juice
⅓ cup sugar
¼ cup butter
⅓ cup brown sugar
⅓ cup all-purpose flour
¾ cup quick-cooking oats

1. Put blueberries into a greased deep baking dish. Drizzle with lemon juice and sprinkle with sugar.
2. Cream butter with brown sugar; mix in flour and oats. Spread mixture over blueberries.
3. Bake at 375°F 35 to 40 minutes. Serve hot or cold with *plain* or *whipped cream*.

*6 TO 8 SERVINGS*

# PRINCE EDWARD ISLAND

CHARLOTTETOWN □

Canada's smallest province is bountifully endowed; its rich, red loam and temperate climate have earned it the soubriquet "Garden of the Gulf." It is also called the Million-Acre Farm, and that is indeed what it is. Prince Edward Island produces the finest seed potatoes in the world and its excellent dairy products are well known.

This little island province is also famous for its fish, particularly shellfish. Oyster farming is an efficient industry in Malpeque Bay and elsewhere, and, when faced with a bucket of oysters, one often has difficulty deciding how to serve them, they are so good in so many ways. Many people feel that they are best served raw on the half-shell with a nippy cocktail sauce, such as one made with ½ cup chili sauce, ⅓ cup ketchup, ⅓ cup prepared horseradish, and 1½ teaspoons Worcestershire sauce. Others think they are best deep-fried, and oyster pie is very popular, too. So, too, are scalloped oysters and oyster soufflé. We chose to include a recipe for oyster bisque, which also used the Island's excellent milk and butter.

Fresh lobsters present a similar problem because of the variety of ways in which they can be served. They may be steamed or boiled, eaten hot or cold, broiled, or made into casseroles or salads. Lobster thermidor is one of the dressiest of many delicious recipes.

Mackerel, another of the island's well-known products, has a special flavor, and soused mackerel is a favorite recipe in the Atlantic provinces.

---

## SPREADS FOR CANAPÉS

*As a base for the following spreads use slices of bread toasted on one side only and crusts removed. Cut slices into interesting shapes and spread untoasted sides lightly with softened butter, then with desired mixture.*

### TOMATO-OLIVE SPREAD

| | |
|---|---|
| 1 medium-sized ripe tomato, peeled | 1 teaspoon finely chopped chives |
| 8 oz. cream cheese, softened | ½ teaspoon salt |
| 2 tablespoons chopped ripe olives | 2 drops Tabasco |

1. Cut tomato into pieces; drain on absorbent paper. Put into a bowl and mash with a fork.
2. Blend in remaining ingredients; chill.

**ABOUT 1⅓ CUPS SPREAD**

## HERB-PARSLEY BUTTER

⅔ cup firm butter
¼ teaspoon onion salt

⅔ cup finely cut parsley
2 teaspoons crushed basil

1. Beat butter with onion salt until fluffy. Add parsley and basil and beat just until blended.
2. Spread on prepared toast bases.

ABOUT 1 CUP BUTTER

NOTE: If desired, sprinkle canapés with *chopped salted pecans.*

PARSLEY BUTTER: Follow recipe for Herb-Parsley Butter. Substitute ¾ *teaspoon seasoned salt* for the onion salt; omit basil.

## ZIPPY CHEESE SPREAD

1 jar (5 oz.) process cheese spread with relish
1 jar (5 oz.) process cheese spread with bacon

2 teaspoons grated onion
⅛ teaspoon dry mustard
2 drops Tabasco

Mix cheese spreads with remaining ingredients until well blended; beat until fluffy.

ABOUT 1⅓ CUPS SPREAD

NOTE: If desired, spread above mixture on prepared toast bases; garnish with *pimiento-stuffed olive slices* or *pimiento strips.* Heat under broiler until cheese is tinged with brown. Serve at once.

## MALPEQUE OYSTER BISQUE

2 cups oysters
1 cup water
1 onion, minced
2 tablespoons butter
2 tablespoons flour

3 cups milk
Salt and pepper
3 tablespoons minced parsley
1 tablespoon butter

1. Simmer oysters in water until edges curl. Drain, reserving liquid. Chop oysters fine.
2. Sauté onion in 2 tablespoons butter. Add flour; stir well. Add 1 cup milk; bring to boiling and cook-stir until smooth. Add remaining milk, oysters, salt and pepper to taste, and parsley. Heat in a double boiler 15 to 20 minutes.
3. Just before serving, stir in 1 tablespoon butter. Sprinkle with *paprika.*     ABOUT 6 SERVINGS

## POTATO SOUP SUPREME

4 medium-sized (about 1½ lbs.) potatoes, cut in ¼-in. slices
4 cups cold water
1 stalk celery, finely cut
1 onion, chopped

1 pimiento, minced
1 teaspoon salt
⅛ teaspoon white pepper
2 beef bouillon cubes
1 cup dairy sour cream
Chopped fresh dill or parsley

1. Put potatoes into a 3-quart saucepan or saucepot with the cold water. Cover and bring to boiling. Add the celery, onion, pimiento, salt, and pepper. Bring to boiling, reduce heat and simmer 1 hour.
2. Remove from heat and drain, reserving liquid. Force vegetables through a sieve into the broth. Return to saucepan. Add the bouillon cubes and stir until dissolved.
3. Shortly before serving, put the sour cream into a bowl. Gradually add 1 cup of the hot soup, stirring constantly. Immediately blend into the remaining soup. Set over low heat just until heated (do not boil).
4. Serve at once, with a sprinkling of dill.

ABOUT 1 QUART SOUP

## HOLIDAY CHICKEN À LA KING

⅓ cup butter
½ cup finely chopped onion
½ cup chopped celery
½ cup chopped green pepper
¼ cup all-purpose flour
1½ teaspoons seasoned salt
⅛ teaspoon pepper

1 can (10 oz.) condensed cream of mushroom soup
3 cups milk
2 cans (4½ oz.) small whole oysters, drained
1 can (5 oz.) whole mushrooms, drained
3 cups diced cooked chicken
¼ cup chopped pimiento

1. Heat butter in a large saucepan. Sauté onion, celery, and green pepper until tender. Blend in flour, salt, and pepper; heat until bubbly.
2. Combine soup and milk; add gradually to mixture in saucepan, stirring until blended. Bring to boiling over medium heat, stirring constantly. Add remaining ingredients and mix well. Cover and heat thoroughly over low heat.
3. Serve over *rice* or *noodles* or in *puff pastry shells.*     ABOUT 10 SERVINGS

## SOUSED MACKEREL

| | |
|---|---|
| 2 lbs. mackerel or herring | 1 tablespoon mixed pickling spices |
| 1 cup vinegar | 1 teaspoon salt |
| 2 thin slices onion | ½ cup water |

1. Fillet and skin fish; cut into 6 pieces. Put fish into a baking dish. Add vinegar, onion, spices, salt, and water. Cover dish.
2. Bake at 350°F 20 to 30 minutes. Serve hot or cold. ABOUT 4 SERVINGS

## RUSTICO LOBSTER THERMIDOR

| | |
|---|---|
| 2 boiled lobsters (about 1½ lbs. each) | Pinch of paprika |
| ⅔ cup sliced mushrooms | 1½ cups milk |
| 3 tablespoons butter | ¼ cup finely grated cheese |
| 3 tablespoons flour | 3 tablespoons sherry |
| ¼ teaspoon salt | 2 tablespoons finely grated cheese |
| ⅛ teaspoon dry mustard | |

1. Cut lobsters in half lengthwise. Remove meat from body and claws; reserve body shells. Cut meat into bite-size chunks.
2. Sauté mushrooms in 1 tablespoon butter. Put remaining butter into top of a double boiler. Stir in flour, salt, dry mustard, and paprika. Add milk gradually, stirring until smooth. Bring to boiling; cook-stir until thickened. Mix in ¼ cup grated cheese, lobster, mushrooms, and sherry. Heat over boiling water until piping hot.
3. Spoon into reserved lobster shells. Sprinkle with remaining cheese.
4. Broil about 2 minutes, or until cheese is golden brown. 4 SERVINGS

## SCALLOPED OYSTERS

| | |
|---|---|
| 1½ qts. oysters | 3 eggs, hard-cooked and sliced |
| 3 tablespoons butter or margarine | 1 teaspoon salt |
| 2 cups soft bread crumbs | ¼ teaspoon pepper |
| ½ cup butter or margarine | Milk |
| ½ cup chopped onion | 4 oz. sharp Cheddar cheese, shredded |
| ½ cup diced celery | |
| 1 clove garlic, minced | |

1. Drain oysters, reserving liquor in a 2-cup measuring cup. Pick over oysters and remove any shell particles. Set oysters aside.
2. Heat 3 tablespoons butter in a skillet. Add the bread crumbs and toss until crumbs are golden brown; set aside.
3. Heat ½ cup butter in the skillet. Add onion, celery, and garlic; cook until onion is transparent.
4. Add drained oysters and heat over low heat, moving and turning constantly, until they are plump, about 4 minutes. Set aside.
5. Spoon one-third of the buttered bread crumbs into a greased 2-quart casserole. Cover with half of the oyster mixture. Top with half of the hard-cooked egg slices. Sprinkle with half of a mixture of salt and pepper. Repeat layering. Top with the remaining bread crumbs.
6. Add enough milk to the reserved oyster liquor to make 2 cups. Pour evenly over the contents of the casserole. Sprinkle the cheese over the top.
7. Bake at 350°F 25 to 30 minutes, or until mixture is bubbly. 8 SERVINGS

## SEAFOOD RAMEKINS

| | |
|---|---|
| 1 cup fine dry bread crumbs, buttered | 1½ cups milk |
| ¼ cup shredded sharp Cheddar cheese | 1½ cups dairy sour cream |
| ¼ cup butter or margarine | 1 can (6½ oz.) crab meat, drained and separated in pieces (bony tissue removed) |
| ¼ cup minced onion | |
| ¼ cup flour | 1 can (5½ oz.) shrimp, drained and cut in half lengthwise |
| ½ teaspoon salt | |
| ⅛ teaspoon pepper | |
| 1½ teaspoons dry mustard | 2 tablespoons chopped parsley |
| Few grains cayenne pepper | |

1. Toss the buttered bread crumbs and cheese together. Set aside.
2. Heat butter in a saucepan; add onion and cook until onion is transparent.
3. Blend in a mixture of flour, salt, pepper, dry mustard, and cayenne pepper; heat until bubbly. Gradually stir in the milk and bring to boiling; cook-stir 1 to 2 minutes.
4. Remove from heat; stirring vigorously, add sour cream in very small amounts; cook and stir 2 to 3 minutes until sauce is just heated.
5. Mix the crab meat, shrimp, and parsley into the sauce.
6. Turn half of mixture into 6 greased ramekins or individual baking dishes. Sprinkle each with

about 2 tablespoons of the crumb mixture.

7. Spoon remaining mixture into ramekins and top with remaining crumbs.

8. Bake at 375°F 20 to 25 minutes, or until crumbs are lightly browned.     6 SERVINGS

## SCALLOP NOODLE BAKE

1 tablespoon butter or margarine
2 tablespoons finely chopped onion
1⅔ cups undiluted evaporated milk
1 tablespoon Worcester-shire sauce
1 teaspoon dry mustard

½ teaspoon salt
8 oz. Cheddar cheese, shredded
1 lb. scallops, cooked and halved
8 oz. noodles (about 4 cups), cooked and drained

1. Melt butter in saucepan; add onion and cook only until transparent.

2. Heat evaporated milk to simmering; gradually add to cooked onion, stirring constantly, and simmer about 3 minutes.

3. Add Worcestershire sauce, dry mustard, salt, and cheese; stir until cheese is melted. Mix in the scallops and drained noodles. Turn into a 1½-quart casserole. Sprinkle with *paprika*.

4. Bake at 350°F about 20 minutes.     6 SERVINGS

## HAM-CHEESE SCALLOP

3 tablespoons flour
½ teaspoon salt
¼ cup butter
2 cups milk
2 cups shredded sharp Cheddar cheese
7 oz. elbow macaroni, cooked and drained

1½ cups cubed cooked ham
2 tablespoons prepared horseradish
2 teaspoons prepared mustard

1. Blend flour and salt into hot butter in a saucepan. Heat until bubbly. Remove from heat; add milk gradually, stirring constantly. Bring to boiling; cook 1 to 2 minutes.

2. Remove from heat. Add cheese all at one time and stir until cheese is melted. Stir in macaroni. Turn mixture into a buttered 1½-quart casserole.

3. Spoon a mixture of ham, horseradish, and mustard evenly over top and press slightly.

4. Heat in a 350°F oven 20 to 25 minutes, or until bubbly.     ABOUT 6 SERVINGS

## SPECIAL NOODLE CASSEROLE

4 oz. (about 2 cups) fine egg noodles
1 cup large-curd cottage cheese
1 cup dairy sour cream
⅓ cup finely chopped onion
1 clove garlic, minced

1 teaspoon Worcester-shire sauce
4 drops Tabasco
1 to 2 tablespoons flour
¼ teaspoon salt
⅛ teaspoon ground white pepper
¼ cup buttered fine dry bread crumbs

1. Cook noodles following package directions; drain.

2. Combine cottage cheese, sour cream, onion, garlic, Worcestershire sauce, and Tabasco. Blend in flour, salt, and pepper; mix with cheese.

3. Combine cheese mixture and noodles. Turn into a greased 1½-quart casserole. Sprinkle crumbs over the top.

4. Set in a 350°F oven about 15 minutes, or until bubbly.     ABOUT 8 SERVINGS

NOTE: If a heartier casserole is desired, alternate layers of the noodle mixture and slices of cooked ham.

## HASH BROWN POTATOES AU GRATIN

1 pkg. (2 lbs.) frozen chopped hash brown potatoes, partially defrosted
1½ teaspoons salt
Few grains pepper
¼ cup coarsely chopped green pepper
1 jar (2 oz.) sliced pimientos, drained and chopped

2 cups milk
¾ cup fine dry bread crumbs
⅓ cup soft butter
⅔ cup shredded pasteurized process sharp cheese

1. Turn potatoes into a buttered shallow 2-quart baking dish, separating into pieces. Sprinkle with salt and pepper. Add green pepper and pimientos; mix lightly. Pour milk over potatoes. Cover with aluminum foil.

2. Cook in a 350°F oven 1¼ hours, or until potatoes are fork-tender. Remove foil; stir potatoes gently. Mix bread crumbs, butter, and cheese. Spoon over top of potatoes. Return to oven and heat 15 minutes, or until cheese is melted.     ABOUT 6 SERVINGS

## CHARLOTTETOWN POTATO PANCAKES

¼ cup finely chopped
  pork
¼ cup finely chopped
  bacon
1 onion, finely chopped

4 potatoes, grated
1 egg
¼ cup flour
Salt and pepper
  to taste

1.  Fry pork, bacon, and onion. Mix in potatoes, egg, flour, and seasonings.
2.  Drop by tablespoonfuls onto a well-greased skillet and brown on both sides.

12 TO 16 PANCAKES

## SCALLOPED SWEET POTATOES AND APPLES

6 medium sweet
  potatoes, washed
1½ cups apple slices
1 tablespoon lemon
  juice

½ cup firmly packed
  brown sugar
¼ cup butter or
  margarine
½ cup apple juice

1.  Cook sweet potatoes in boiling salted water to cover until almost tender; drain. Peel potatoes and cut into crosswise slices, ¼ inch thick.
2.  Toss apples with lemon juice.
3.  Butter a 1½-quart baking dish. Arrange half of the sweet potatoes in bottom and cover with half of the apple slices. Sprinkle with half of brown sugar. Dot with 2 tablespoons of the butter. Repeat layering. Pour apple juice over all.
4.  Bake at 350°F about 45 minutes.

ABOUT 6 SERVINGS

## MUSHROOM DELIGHT

1 lb. fresh mushrooms,
  sliced
½ clove garlic, minced
2 tablespoons minced
  parsley

½ teaspoon salt
⅛ teaspoon pepper
¼ cup butter or
  margarine
1 cup dairy sour cream
1 tablespoon flour

1.  Add mushrooms, garlic, parsley, salt, and pepper to hot butter in a skillet. Cook, stirring occasionally, until mushrooms are tender and lightly browned.
2.  Add to the skillet a mixture of sour cream and flour. Stir and cook about 5 minutes, or until sauce is slightly thicker and thoroughly heated (do not boil).
3.  Serve on *croutons* or *toast points*.    6 SERVINGS

## SALMON-STUFFED POTATOES

4 large baking potatoes
  (about 2½ lbs.)
Fat
⅔ cup undiluted
  evaporated milk
2 tablespoons butter
1 teaspoon salt
⅛ teaspoon white pepper

⅓ cup chopped green
  pepper
2 tablespoons chopped
  onion
1 cup canned salmon,
  flaked
½ cup shredded sharp
  Cheddar cheese

1.  Wash, scrub, and dry potatoes. Rub with fat; prick with a fork.
2.  Bake at 425°F about 1 hour, or until soft.
3.  Cut a thin slice from top of each potato. Scoop out potatoes and mash thoroughly. Stir in milk, butter, salt, pepper, green pepper, and onion; beat well. Mix in salmon and cheese. Spoon mixture into potato shells.
4.  Return potatoes to oven and heat 15 minutes.

4 SERVINGS

## APPLE CABBAGE SLAW

¼ cup dairy sour
  cream
1 teaspoon lemon juice
1 teaspoon prepared
  horseradish
1 teaspoon sugar
½ teaspoon salt

⅛ teaspoon white
  pepper
1 cup finely diced,
  pared apples
1 cup finely shredded
  cabbage

1.  Blend sour cream, lemon juice, horseradish, sugar, salt and pepper. Chill thoroughly.
2.  When ready to serve slaw, pour chilled dressing over apples and cabbage and toss to coat. If desired, serve on cabbage leaves.    4 TO 6 SERVINGS

## WHIPPED CREAM CAKE

1½ cups sifted cake
  flour
1 cup sugar
2 teaspoons baking
  powder
¼ teaspoon salt

1 cup chilled heavy
  cream, whipped to soft
  peaks
1½ teaspoons vanilla
  extract
¼ teaspoon lemon
  extract
2 eggs, well beaten

1.  Sift the cake flour, sugar, baking powder, and salt together; set aside.
2.  Fold whipped cream, extracts, and beaten eggs

together. Sift about one fourth of the dry ingredients at a time over the cream mixture, gently folding until just blended after each addition. Turn into 2 prepared 8-inch layer cake pans and spread evenly to edges.

3. Bake at 350°F 30 minutes, or until cake tests done.

4. Cool and remove from pans. Fill and frost as desired. TWO 8-INCH CAKE LAYERS

## BAKED APPLE AND CHEESE DESSERT

| | |
|---|---|
| 5 cups pared apple slices | ¼ teaspoon ground mace |
| 1 tablespoon lemon juice | ½ cup firmly packed brown sugar |
| ¼ cup firmly packed brown sugar | ¼ cup butter or margarine |
| ½ cup all-purpose flour | 1 cup shredded sharp Cheddar cheese |
| ¼ teaspoon salt | |
| ½ teaspoon ground cinnamon | |

1. Arrange apple slices in a 1¼-quart shallow baking dish. Sprinkle with lemon juice and ¼ cup of brown sugar.

2. Combine flour, salt, spices, and ½ cup brown sugar. Cut in butter until mixture is crumbly. Mix in cheese. Spoon over apples and press lightly.

3. Bake at 350°F about 35 minutes, or until apples are tender. Serve warm with *cream.*

ABOUT 6 SERVINGS

## APPLE DATE DESSERT

| | |
|---|---|
| ½ cup butter or margarine | 1 teaspoon ground nutmeg |
| 2 cups sugar | 3 cups grated, pared apples (3 large) |
| 2 eggs | |
| 2 cups sifted cake flour | 2 tablespoons lemon juice |
| 1 teaspoon baking soda | |
| ½ teaspoon salt | 1 cup chopped nuts |
| 1½ teaspoons ground cinnamon | 1 cup chopped dates |

1. Cream butter and sugar until light and fluffy. Add eggs, one at a time, beating thoroughly after each addition.

2. Sift cake flour, baking soda, salt, and spices together. Mix apples and lemon juice. Add dry ingredients alternately with apples to creamed mixture, beating until blended after each addition. Fold in nuts and dates.

3. Turn mixture into a greased and floured 13x9x2-inch pan and spread evenly.

4. Bake at 350°F 50 to 55 minutes. Serve topped with *sweetened whipped cream.* ABOUT 12 SERVINGS

## CAVENDISH APPLE CARAMEL

| | |
|---|---|
| 6 apples, cored, pared, and cut in half | ½ cup all-purpose flour |
| ½ cup butter | ¼ teaspoon salt |
| 1 cup brown sugar | 1 cup chopped nuts |

1. Arrange the apple halves in a buttered shallow baking dish.

2. Cream butter and brown sugar. Mix in flour, salt, and nuts. Spread mixture over apples.

3. Bake at 375°F 30 minutes. Serve hot with *plain or whipped cream.* ABOUT 6 SERVINGS

## CREAMY CRUMB-TOP APPLE PIE

| | |
|---|---|
| 1 cup sugar | ⅛ teaspoon salt |
| 4 teaspoons flour | 1 unbaked 9-in. pie shell |
| ½ teaspoon ground cinnamon | 6 large cooking apples |
| | Crumb Topping, *below* |
| ½ teaspoon ground nutmeg | ½ cup heavy cream |

1. Combine the sugar, flour, cinnamon, nutmeg, and salt; mix well. Sprinkle 2 tablespoons of mixture over bottom of unbaked pie shell. Set remaining mixture aside.

2. Wash, quarter, core, pare, and thinly slice apples. Turn into pie shell, heaping slightly at center. Sprinkle with remaining sugar mixture.

3. Sprinkle Crumb Topping over apples.

4. Bake at 450°F 10 minutes; reduce oven temperature to 350°F and bake 25 to 30 minutes, or until apples are tender.

5. Set on wire rack. Pour cream evenly over top of pie. Let stand about 15 minutes. Serve while still warm. ONE 9-INCH PIE

**CRUMB TOPPING:** Mix ¼ *cup packed brown sugar, 3 tablespoons flour, 1 tablespoon sugar, ⅛ teaspoon ground cinnamon, ⅛ teaspoon ground nutmeg,* and ⅛ *teaspoon salt.* Cut in ¼ *cup butter or margarine* until mixture is crumbly.

# NOVA SCOTIA

HALIFAX

There are many wonderful things to be said about Nova Scotia fare, for this province is blessed with many beautiful foods. It is also fortunate in having the traditions of three types of cooking.

Among the foods are, of course, both fresh and saltwater fish, including many kinds of shellfish; fruits, particularly apples, for which the Annapolis Valley is famous, and cranberries and wild strawberries of exquisite flavor which are gathered commercially; maple syrup; fresh vegetables; and dairy products.

Traditional recipes brought by French, Scots, and German settlers and adapted to the local foods have been blended into a varied cuisine.

In Cape Breton Island the Scottish tradition is very strong, and even today in out-of-the-way fishing villages and farms, Gaelic is spoken. The French tradition was established in the area on the western shores of the Minas Basin, where the early French settlers of 1675 took land on the banks of four tidal rivers, Gaspereau, Cornwallis, Canard, and Habitant. Here they built dykes to keep out the salt water and started growing apples. Expelled from Acadia in 1755, many of

them returned to Nova Scotia after 1763, and their descendants are now living in various parts of the province, particularly from Margaree Harbour to Cap Rouge along the Cabot Trail on Cape Breton Island.

The third national culinary tradition was brought to Lunenburg more than two centuries ago by a group of Germans who became subjects of the British Crown after the accession of George I, Elector of Hanover. Throughout the years they have managed to maintain their distinctive dialect, culture, and many recipes.

## SOLOMON GUNDY

| 6 salt herring | ¼ cup sugar |
| 1 large onion, thinly sliced | 2 tablespoons whole mixed pickling |
| 3 cups white wine vinegar | spice (including bay leaves) |

1.  Wash herring under running water to remove

♦ 59

salt. Trim off heads and tails; soak in cold water overnight.

2. Next day, drain and fillet fish; cut into 2-inch pieces. Pack layers of fish pieces and onion slices into wide-mouth jars.

3. Combine vinegar, sugar, and spices; simmer 5 minutes. Cool and pour over herring to cover. Refrigerate 4 to 6 days before serving.

## APPETIZER MEATBALLS

| | |
|---|---|
| 3 tablespoons finely chopped onion | ⅛ teaspoon white pepper |
| 2 tablespoons butter | ⅛ teaspoon ground allspice |
| ½ lb. lean ground beef | |
| ½ lb. lean ground veal | 1 egg, beaten |
| ½ lb. lean ground pork | ¾ cup cream |
| 2 cooked medium potatoes, sieved | ¼ cup water |
| | Flour |
| 1½ teaspoons salt | 2 to 3 tablespoons butter |

1. Brown onion until golden in 2 tablespoons heated butter in a large skillet.

2. Lightly mix in a bowl the meat, potatoes, onion, and a mixture of the salt, pepper, and allspice. Add the egg, cream, and water, mixing thoroughly. Shape into ¾- to 1-inch balls and coat with flour.

3. Brown 2 to 3 tablespoons butter in the skillet. Add meatballs and brown on all sides.

4. Transfer meatballs to a chafing dish and keep hot. Provide fancy cocktail picks for spearing them.

ABOUT 8 DOZEN MEATBALLS

## STRAWBERRY COFFEE RING

*For brunch, generously sift confectioners' (icing) sugar over the top. For luncheon, top with a whipped dessert topping blended with crushed ripe strawberries.*

| | |
|---|---|
| 1 pt. ripe strawberries, rinsed and hulled | 1 egg, beaten |
| | ½ cup milk |
| 1¾ cups all-purpose flour | ⅓ cup sugar |
| | 1 tablespoon flour |
| 1 tablespoon sugar | 1 teaspoon ground cardamom |
| 1 teaspoon baking powder | |
| | 1 egg yolk, beaten |
| 1 teaspoon salt | 1 tablespoon water |
| ⅓ cup firm butter or margarine | |

1. Spread the hulled strawberries on absorbent paper to dry thoroughly.

2. Blend the flour, sugar, baking powder, and salt in a bowl. Cut in the butter with a pastry blender or two knives until particles become the size of rice kernels.

3. Combine the egg and milk. Add all at one time to the dry ingredients. Stir with a fork until dough follows fork. Form dough into a ball. (If necessary, chill dough until easy to handle.) Roll out dough on a lightly floured surface into a 15x10-inch rectangle; set aside while preparing strawberries.

4. Quarter strawberries and toss gently with a mixture of the ⅓ cup sugar, 1 tablespoon flour, and the cardamom. Spoon strawberry mixture over dough. Beginning with longer side, roll dough as for jelly roll; press edge to seal. Transfer to a shallow baking pan, placing sealed edge down. Join the ends to form a ring, pressing slightly to seal ends. With scissors, snip at equal intervals through ring almost to center.

5. Brush top evenly with a mixture of the egg yolk and water.

6. Bake at 375°F 30 to 35 minutes. Serve warm.

1 COFFEE CAKE RING

## COTTAGE FRITTERS

| | |
|---|---|
| 1 cup all-purpose flour | 2 cups dry cottage cheese, sieved |
| ½ teaspoon salt | |
| ⅛ teaspoon freshly ground pepper | 3 egg yolks |
| | 2 teaspoons salt |
| 1 tablespoon butter, melted | ½ teaspoon mace |
| | 2 tablespoons flour |
| ⅔ cup milk | 2 cups crushed, bite-size rice cereal |
| 1 tablespoon lemon juice | |
| | Fat for deep frying, heated to 370°F |
| 1 egg yolk | |
| 1 egg white | Egg Sauce, *below* |

1. For batter, sift 1 cup flour, ½ teaspoon salt, and pepper together. Add melted butter, milk, lemon juice, and 1 egg yolk; blend well.

2. Set aside until batter comes to room temperature. Beat egg white until stiff and fold into batter.

3. For fritters, beat cottage cheese, 3 egg yolks, 2 teaspoons salt, mace, and 2 tablespoons flour together. Drop a tablespoonful at a time into batter, then into crushed cereal, coating thoroughly.

4. Fry one layer of balls at a time in the hot fat until lightly browned. Serve hot with Egg Sauce.

6 TO 8 SERVINGS

**EGG SAUCE:** Heat *2 tablespoons butter* in a saucepan. Mix in *2 tablespoons flour*, ¼ *teaspoon salt*, and ⅛ *teaspoon pepper*; heat until bubbly. Add *1 cup milk* gradually, stirring until smooth. Bring to boiling and cook 1 to 2 minutes, stirring constantly. Mix in *2 hard-cooked eggs*, chopped.

ABOUT 1¼ CUPS SAUCE

## BAKED HALIBUT SUPERB

| | |
|---|---|
| ½ cup fine Melba toast crumbs | 1 can (4 oz.) mushroom stems and pieces, drained |
| ¼ cup butter or margarine, melted | 2 lbs. fresh or frozen halibut fillets, cut into 12 pieces |
| ⅔ cup minced scallions or green onions | |
| 2 tablespoons snipped parsley | 2 tablespoons butter or margarine |
| ½ teaspoon poultry seasoning | 2 tablespoons flour |
| ½ lb. fresh or frozen scallops, chopped | ¼ teaspoon salt |
| | Few grains pepper |
| | 1 cup milk |
| | Shredded Parmesan cheese |

1. Toss the crumbs and melted butter together in a bowl. Add the scallions, parsley, poultry seasoning, scallops, and mushrooms and mix well.
2. Place a piece of halibut in the bottom of each of six ramekins. Spoon stuffing mixture over fish and top with remaining halibut pieces.
3. Heat butter in a saucepan. Stir in flour, salt, and pepper and cook until bubbly. Stir in the milk and bring rapidly to boiling; stir and cook 1 to 2 minutes.
4. Spoon sauce over halibut. Sprinkle with Parmesan cheese.
5. Bake at 350°F. 20 to 25 minutes. If desired, before serving, set ramekins under broiler with tops about 3 inches from source of heat until lightly browned; watch carefully to avoid overbrowning.

6 SERVINGS

## DIGBY SCALLOPS

| | |
|---|---|
| 1 cup fine bread crumbs | 1 egg |
| ½ teaspoon salt | 2 tablespoons water |
| Few grains *each* pepper and cayenne pepper | 1½ lbs. scallops |
| | ¼ cup melted butter |
| | Tartar Sauce, *below* |

1. Mix bread crumbs, salt, pepper, and cayenne.
2. Beat egg with a fork and mix in water. Dip each

scallop first in bread crumbs, then in egg mixture, and again in crumbs.
3. Put breaded scallops into a baking dish and let stand about 30 minutes for coating to set.
4. Pour melted butter over scallops.
5. Bake at 450°F 30 minutes, or until crisp and brown. Serve with Tartar Sauce. ABOUT 6 SERVINGS

### TARTAR SAUCE

| | |
|---|---|
| 1 medium dill pickle | 1½ tablespoons prepared mustard |
| 1 tablespoon capers | 1 cup mayonnaise |
| 3 sprigs parsley, snipped | |
| ½ small onion, finely chopped | |

Chop pickle and capers very finely; mix with parsley, onion, mustard, and mayonnaise.

ABOUT 1½ CUPS SAUCE

## FISH FILLET TWIRLS WITH CELERY STUFFING

| | |
|---|---|
| 2 lbs. frozen fish fillets (6 fillets needed), thawed | 2 cups soft bread crumbs |
| Lemon juice | 2 eggs, beaten |
| 3 tablespoons butter | ½ cup cream |
| ½ cup diced celery | 1 tablespoon minced parsley |
| 2 tablespoons chopped green pepper | ½ teaspoon thyme |
| 1 tablespoon finely chopped onion | ⅛ teaspoon celery salt |
| | Pinch ground nutmeg |
| | ¼ teaspoon salt |
| | Few grains pepper |

1. Sprinkle fish fillets with lemon juice. Fit each fillet around the inside of a well-greased muffin-pan well.
2. Heat butter in a large skillet. Mix in celery, green pepper, and onion; cook until celery is tender. Remove from heat.
3. Add bread crumbs to skillet and toss to mix well. Combine eggs, cream, parsley, thyme, celery salt, nutmeg, salt, and pepper; add to bread crumb mixture and stir in. Set over low heat until thoroughly heated, stirring occasionally.
4. Spoon stuffing into fish twirls.
5. Bake at 350°F about 20 minutes, or until fish flakes easily when tested with a fork.
6. Remove fish twirls from wells by running a knife around edges and lifting them out with a spoon. Serve immediately. 6 SERVINGS

## LUNENBURG SAUSAGE

| | |
|---|---|
| 10 lbs. ground pork | ¼ cup coriander |
| 7½ lbs. ground beef | 1 tablespoon allspice |
| 2 tablespoons salt | ½ tablespoon savory |
| 2 oz. pepper | |

1. Mix ground meat, salt, and ground seasonings.
2. Wrap and store in refrigerator. This sausage may be frozen in small amounts.

## HERB-BUTTERED CORN AND BEANS

| | |
|---|---|
| 2 cans (10 oz. each) niblet corn | ½ teaspoon salt |
| 1 can (14 oz.) cut green beans | ¼ teaspoon ground sage |
| ¼ cup butter or margarine | ⅛ teaspoon thyme |
| ¼ cup chopped onion | ⅛ teaspoon marjoram |
| | ⅛ teaspoon pepper |

1. Drain vegetables and set aside. Reserve liquid for other use.
2. Heat butter in a saucepan. Add onion, salt, sage, thyme, marjoram, and pepper. Cook over medium heat until onion is soft, stirring frequently. Add drained corn and beans. Heat thoroughly.

ABOUT 8 SERVINGS

## DUTCH KOHL SLAW

| | |
|---|---|
| ½ lb. clear pork | Salt and pepper |
| 1 cup brown sugar | 1 small cabbage, finely shredded |
| ¾ cup vinegar | |

1. Fry out pork.
2. Add to pork and fat brown sugar, vinegar, salt and pepper to taste, and cabbage; mix well. Simmer 1 hour. Serve hot. ABOUT 8 SERVINGS

## APPLE-CARAWAY SLAW

| | |
|---|---|
| ¼ cup mayonnaise | ½ teaspoon grated onion |
| 1 tablespoon sugar | |
| ½ teaspoon salt | 3 cups finely shredded cabbage |
| 1 tablespoon wine vinegar | 2 red apples, chilled |
| 1 tablespoon prepared mustard | 1 teaspoon caraway seed |

1. Blend the first 6 ingredients and chill.
2. Reserving half of 1 apple for garnish, cut unpared apples into cubes. Combine with cabbage.

Add chilled dressing and caraway seed; toss until well mixed. Turn slaw into serving bowl.
3. Slice reserved apple half into thin lengthwise wedges. Garnish slaw with apple wedges.

6 TO 8 SERVINGS

## BLUEBERRY UPSIDE-DOWN CAKE

| | |
|---|---|
| **Topping:** | 1 teaspoon baking powder |
| ⅓ cup butter or margarine | ½ teaspoon salt |
| ½ cup sugar | 3 egg yolks |
| ⅛ teaspoon salt | ½ cup sugar |
| 2 cups fresh blueberries, rinsed and drained | ⅓ cup orange juice |
| **Cake batter:** | 2 tablespoons lemon juice |
| 1¾ cups sifted cake flour | 3 egg whites |
| | ½ cup sugar |
| | Sweetened whipped cream |

1. For topping, melt butter in a heavy 10-inch skillet with a heat-resistant handle. Blend in sugar and salt. Add blueberries and spread evenly. Set aside.
2. For cake batter, sift the flour, baking powder, and salt together; set aside.
3. Beat egg yolks until thick and lemon colored. Gradually add ½ cup sugar and orange and lemon juices, beating thoroughly. Sift dry ingredients about one fourth at a time over egg yolk mixture and gently fold until just blended after each addition. Set aside.
4. Beat egg whites until frothy. Gradually add sugar, continuing to beat until stiff peaks are formed. Gently fold batter into meringue until just blended. Turn batter into skillet over blueberries, spreading evenly.
5. Bake at 350°F 45 to 50 minutes, or until cake tests done.
6. Using a spatula, loosen cake from sides of skillet and immediately invert onto a serving plate. Allow skillet to remain over cake a few seconds so syrup will drain onto cake. Remove skillet.
7. Serve cake warm, topping each wedge with a spoonful of sweetened whipped cream.

ONE UPSIDE-DOWN CAKE

RASPBERRY UPSIDE-DOWN CAKE: Follow recipe for Blueberry Upside-Down Cake. Substitute *1 pint red raspberries*, rinsed and drained, for the blueberries.

**PEACH UPSIDE-DOWN CAKE:** Follow recipe for Blueberry Upside-Down Cake. In topping, substitute *lightly packed light brown sugar* for granulated sugar. Substitute *4 medium (about 1 pound) firm ripe peaches*, peeled and sliced, for the blueberries.

**STRAWBERRY UPSIDE-DOWN CAKE:** Follow recipe for Peach Upside-Down Cake. Substitute *1 quart fresh ripe strawberries*, rinsed, drained, hulled, and sliced, for the peaches.

## FANCY SCOTCH SHORTBREAD

1 cup butter
½ cup sugar
3½ cups sifted all-purpose flour
Confectioners' sugar

1. Cream butter; add sugar gradually, beating until fluffy.
2. Add flour gradually, mixing only until blended (mixture will be crumbly).
3. Turn dough into a 15x10x1-inch jelly roll pan. Using a spatula, spread cookie dough evenly to fit the pan.
4. Bake at 325°F 45 minutes, or until light golden brown.
5. Remove from oven and immediately cut with cookie cutter into crescents or other interesting shapes. Shortbread must be cut into shapes in the pan while hot. Cool cookies in pan set on wire rack.
6. When cool, remove cookies from pan and sprinkle lightly with confectioners' sugar.

ABOUT 2½ DOZEN COOKIES

## CAPE BRETON OATCAKES

2 cups all-purpose flour
2 cups oats
¼ cup sugar
¼ cup brown sugar
1 teaspoon salt
½ teaspoon baking soda
1 cup butter
Water

1. Mix flour, oats, sugars, salt, and baking soda. Cut in butter. Add water in small amounts, mixing with a fork until dough is of rolling consistency.
2. Roll out dough to ⅛-inch thickness. Cut in triangles.
3. Bake at 350°F 20 minutes.

ABOUT 3½ DOZEN OATCAKES

## ANNAPOLIS CRANBERRY-APPLES

1 cup cranberries
1 cup water
1 cup sugar
6 apples, pared, cored, and cut in eighths

1. Cook cranberries in water until skins burst. Press through a sieve; add sugar and bring to boiling. Add apples and cook slowly until apples are clear and have absorbed the juice.
2. Chill and serve with *whipped cream*.

ABOUT 6 SERVINGS

## ACADIAN BLUEBERRY GRUNT

1 qt. blueberries
½ cup water
½ cup sugar
2 cups all-purpose flour
4 teaspoons baking powder
1 teaspoon sugar
½ teaspoon salt
1 tablespoon *each* butter and shortening
¾ cup milk (about)

1. Combine berries, water, and sugar in a large saucepan; cover and cook until there is plenty of juice.
2. Mix flour, baking powder, sugar, and salt. Cut in butter and shortening, then, mixing with a fork, add enough milk to make a soft dough. Drop by tablespoonfuls onto the hot blueberry sauce. Cover tightly and cook 15 minutes without peeking.
3. Serve hot with *cream*, if desired.

6 TO 8 SERVINGS

## APPLE-CHEESE COBBLER

4 cups sliced apples
⅓ cup sugar
1 tablespoon quick-cooking tapioca
½ teaspoon ground cinnamon
¼ teaspoon salt
¼ cup water
2 tablespoons butter or margarine
⅓ cup milk
1 cup all-purpose biscuit mix
4 oz. sharp Cheddar cheese, shredded

1. Combine apples, sugar, tapioca, cinnamon, salt, water, and butter in a saucepan. Cook over low heat, stirring occasionally, until apples are almost tender.
2. Stir milk into biscuit mix to make a soft dough.
3. Turn dough onto a lightly floured surface and roll into a 10x8-inch rectangle. Sprinkle with cheese. Roll up as for a jelly roll; cut into ½-inch slices.

4. Turn hot apple mixture into a 1½-quart baking dish. Arrange dough slices on top of apples.
5. Bake at 425°F about 20 minutes, or until topping is lightly browned.   ABOUT 6 SERVINGS

## STRAWBERRY BAKED ALASKA PIE

| | |
|---|---|
| 1⅓ cups fine vanilla wafer crumbs | 1¼ cups sugar |
| ¼ cup butter, melted | 1 qt. strawberry ice cream |
| 4 cups fresh rhubarb, cut in 1-in. pieces | 3 egg whites |
| | 6 tablespoons sugar |

1. Mix vanilla wafer crumbs and butter. Turn into a 9-inch pie pan and press evenly. Chill.
2. Combine rhubarb and 1¼ cups sugar in a saucepan. Cook over low heat, stirring occasionally, until sugar is dissolved. Cover and continue cooking until rhubarb is tender. Cool. Chill.
3. Alternately spoon ice cream and 1 cup of rhubarb sauce into prepared shell. Pack down lightly. Wrap and freeze until firm.
4. Beat egg whites until frothy. Add 6 tablespoons sugar gradually, beating until stiff peaks are formed. Spread meringue over ice cream, being sure meringue touches crust all around edge.
5. Bake at 450°F 4 to 5 minutes, or until lightly browned. Serve immediately with remaining rhubarb sauce.   ONE 9-INCH PIE

## MAPLE PRALINES

| | |
|---|---|
| 1 cup maple syrup | Few grains salt |
| 2 cups confectioners' (icing) sugar | 1 tablespoon butter |
| ½ cup undiluted evaporated milk | 1 teaspoon vanilla extract |
| | 1½ cups broken pecans |

1. Mix the syrup, confectioners' sugar, evaporated milk, salt, and butter in a heavy saucepan. Bring to boiling; set a candy thermometer in place. Cook over low heat, stirring occasionally, until thermometer registers 234°F.
2. Remove from heat; remove thermometer. Add vanilla extract and pecans; stir until mixture begins to thicken.
3. Set over a pan of hot water. Quickly drop mixture by spoonfuls onto aluminum foil or buttered waxed paper. Cool until set, then wrap.
ABOUT 1 POUND CANDY

## MAPLE PANOCHA

| | |
|---|---|
| 1 cup granulated sugar | 2 tablespoons corn syrup |
| 1 cup maple sugar | 1 cup cream |
| 2 cups firmly packed brown sugar | 2 tablespoons butter |
| | 1 cup nuts, chopped |

1. Combine sugars, corn syrup, and cream in a saucepan; stir over low heat until sugars are moistened. Set candy thermometer in place.
2. Cook, stirring occasionally, to 238°F.
3. Remove from heat and add butter; cool slightly. Beat until creamy, adding nuts last few minutes. Turn into a buttered pan.
4. When cool, cut into bars or squares.
ABOUT 2½ POUNDS CANDY

## OLD-FASHIONED CAULIFLOWER PICKLES

| | |
|---|---|
| 3 large heads (2½ to 3 lbs. each) cauliflower, rinsed | 2 teaspoons mustard seed |
| Water | 2 teaspoons celery seed |
| 1 qt. white vinegar | 1 teaspoon ground turmeric |
| 2½ cups sugar | 10 whole cloves |
| ½ cup dried onion flakes | 1 dried red pepper |
| 2½ teaspoons salt | 1 can (4 oz.) pimiento, drained and cut in strips |

1. Remove large leaves from cauliflower; break into flowerets.
2. Bring 4 quarts water to boiling in a large saucepot. Add cauliflower. Cover; remove from heat and let stand while preparing the vinegar mixture.
3. Put 1½ quarts water into a large saucepan. Add vinegar, sugar, onion flakes, salt, mustard seed, celery seed, and turmeric. Tie cloves and red pepper in cheesecloth. Add to vinegar mixture. Bring to boiling. Boil, uncovered, 5 minutes.
4. Drain water from cauliflower. Pour hot vinegar mixture over cauliflower. Add pimiento. Return to boiling point and cook about 5 minutes, or until cauliflower is crisp-tender. Remove spice bag.
5. Ladle cauliflower mixture into clean, hot jars. Seal, following manufacturer's directions.
6. Process 15 minutes in boiling water bath.*
7. Cool and store.   ABOUT 5 QUARTS PICKLES
*For a boiling water bath, put a rack in a saucepot and set filled jars on rack. Pour in boiling water to cover 1 or 2 inches above jars. Cover saucepot and bring water to boiling before starting the timing.

# NEWFOUNDLAND

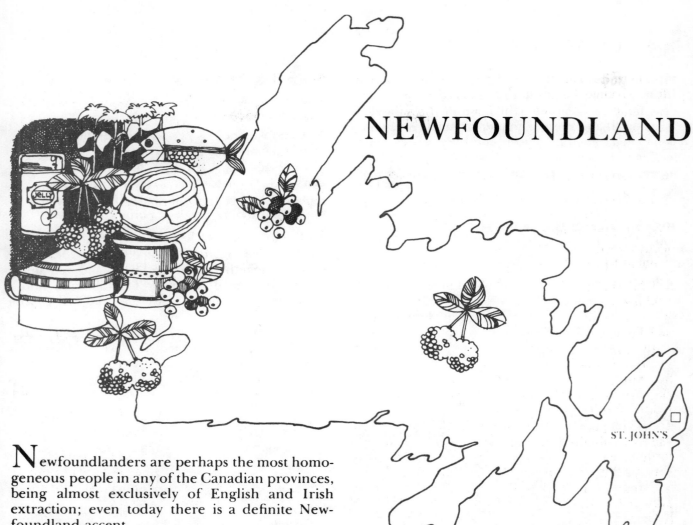

Newfoundlanders are perhaps the most homogeneous people in any of the Canadian provinces, being almost exclusively of English and Irish extraction; even today there is a definite Newfoundland accent.

Fish is, of course, plentiful, for the famous Grand Banks, to which fishermen from many nations have come for centuries, lie on its doorstep. Newfoundlanders have evolved many unique recipes for products of the sea. They are, for instance, some of the very few Canadians in any province who have a sealing industry and, as a delicious by-product of their hunt for fur and seal oil, they have invented flipper pie. When you say "fish" in Newfoundland, it is assumed that you are talking about cod, for cod is available all year round, fresh, dried, or salted. Even the cod's tongue has been put to good use.

Newfoundland has very little arable land, but the rocky barrens and spongy marshes produce many wild berries that are not found elsewhere. Partridge berries, marshberries, squash berries, and bakeapples are some of them.

Probably the favorite food is a boiled dinner, consisting of salt pork or beef cooked with potatoes, turnips, carrots, and cabbage. Fish and brewis is another popular dish, consisting of salt cod, of course, and hard biscuits that are soaked in water, then brought to the boil and drained. Much salt meat and fish is used, and dandelion greens, turnip tops, and cabbage are still cooked with a piece of salt meat for flavor.

## BONAVISTA BAY CODS' TONGUES

| | |
|---|---|
| 24 cod tongues | ½ cup milk or |
| ½ cup all-purpose | 1 egg |
| flour | Fat for frying |
| ½ teaspoon salt | |

1. Rinse tongues and scrape lightly to clean. If tongues are salted, soak them in cold water 10 minutes.
2. Mix flour and salt. Dip tongues in milk and roll in flour.
3. Fry in hot fat 3 to 5 minutes. ABOUT 6 SERVINGS

## HEART'S DELIGHT COD ROE

If the roe is a large winter roe — that is, a roe before spawning — boil it in salted water for about 5 minutes. If the roe is summer or small roe, there is no need to boil it. Cut the *cod roe* in slices, roll it in *flour or cornflake crumbs*, and fry it in *oil* until nicely browned. It can be served with *crisp bacon*.

## FISHERMAN'S STEW WITH FRESH FISH

*This delicious stew is often made by fishermen on the fishing grounds.*

| | |
|---|---|
| 4 slices fat back pork | 2 cups sliced potatoes |
| 3 lbs. fresh cod | Salt and pepper |
| 1 medium onion, sliced | 1 cup boiling water |

1.   Render out pork in a large saucepan.
2.   Clean fish, remove skin, and cut into pieces. Add fish and onion to fat, then add potatoes, seasonings, and boiling water. Cook until potatoes and fish are tender (about 30 minutes).

ABOUT 4 SERVINGS

## PORT AUX BASQUES FLIPPER PIE

During April and May the flippers of young harp seals are used to make pie. Many organizations have flipper pie suppers where pies several feet in diameter and holding 15 to 20 pounds of seal meat and gallons of vegetables are served. The secret of success in making a tasty flipper dish is to see that all the fat is removed, as it has a strong flavor which will permeate the flesh if left on it (many housewives remove the fat with a razor blade). Then wash the *flippers* in water to which *one tablespoon of baking soda* has been added. The soda will turn any fat that is left white, thus making it easier to remove. Render *salt pork* in a roasting pan, and fry the meat, which has been dipped in *seasoned flour*, on both sides. Some cooks use *cinnamon* in the seasoning. Then add a little *water, onions, and parsnips*; these add flavor and sweetness. Cook, covered, until flippers are tender — 1½ to 2 hours, depending on the size. In a separate pot cook *carrots* and *turnips* until partly cooked. Remove the flippers from the pan and put in a casserole. Make *gravy*, pour over the flippers, and add the vegetables. Cover with *pastry* and bake until pastry is cooked. Serve with *partridge berry jam, black currant jelly*, or *lemon slices*.

## CABBAGE AND RICE CASSEROLE

| | |
|---|---|
| 3 cups shredded cabbage (about ¾ lb.) | 2 tablespoons butter or margarine |
| ¾ cup cooked rice | ½ cup shredded sharp Cheddar cheese |
| 4 slices bacon, fried and crumbled | ¼ teaspoon salt |
| 1 can (8 oz.) tomato sauce | Few grains pepper |
| 1 teaspoon sugar | ½ cup fine dry bread crumbs, buttered |

1.   Cook cabbage, loosely covered, in a large amount of boiling *salted water* 3 minutes; drain.
2.   Toss together cabbage, rice, and remaining ingredients except crumbs. Turn mixture into a lightly greased 1-quart casserole. Top evenly with buttered crumbs.
3.   Heat in a 350°F oven 25 minutes, or until crumbs are lightly browned.   ABOUT 4 SERVINGS

## SPECIAL CARROTS

| | |
|---|---|
| 1 lb. tender young carrots, pared | 2 tablespoons heavy cream |
| 2 tablespoons water | 1 tablespoon melted butter or margarine |
| 2 tablespoons butter or margarine | 1 tablespoon finely minced parsley |
| 1 teaspoon sugar | ⅛ teaspoon crushed thyme or ground ginger |
| ¼ teaspoon salt | |
| 1 egg yolk | |

1.   Use carrots whole and trim to about the same length (cut into 4-inch lengths if carrots are large). Put into a small skillet with the water, butter, sugar, and salt. Cover tightly and bring to boiling. Cook over low heat 15 minutes, or until crisp-tender; shake frequently.
2.   Meanwhile, mix egg yolk and remaining ingredients until blended. Add to cooked carrots in skillet; mix gently. Remove from heat; stir until the curd coats carrots, about 2 minutes.   4 SERVINGS

## BLUEBERRY APRICOT NECTAR MOLD

| | |
|---|---|
| 1 env. unflavored gelatin | 1 pkg. (4 oz.) cream cheese, softened |
| 1½ cups apricot nectar | ½ cup dairy sour cream |
| 1 tablespoon lemon juice | 1½ cups fresh blueberries |
| ¼ teaspoon salt | |

1.   Soften gelatin in ¼ cup apricot nectar.

2. Heat remaining nectar to boiling; add gelatin and stir until dissolved. Stir in lemon juice and salt. Chill until slightly thickened.
3. Beat cheese until light; blend in sour cream. Add gelatin mixture gradually, beating until smooth. Chill until slightly thicker. Mix in blueberries.
4. Turn into a 3-cup mold or 6 individual molds. Chill until firm.
5. Unmold and serve on crisp *salad greens*.

6 SERVINGS

## CREAMY PERFECTION SALAD

| | |
|---|---|
| 2 tablespoons unflavored gelatin | ¼ teaspoon Worcester-shire sauce |
| ¾ cup sugar | ½ teaspoon celery seed |
| ¼ teaspoon salt | 1 cup thinly sliced cabbage |
| 2½ cups water | 1 cup thinly sliced celery |
| 1 cup dairy sour cream | ½ cup slivered green pepper |
| ¼ cup lemon juice | 1 cup coarsely shredded carrot |
| 2 tablespoons white vinegar | 2 tablespoons sliced pimiento-stuffed olives |
| 2 tablespoons drained prepared horseradish | |
| 1 teaspoon grated onion | |

1. Mix gelatin, sugar, and salt in a saucepan; add 1 cup of the water. Stir over low heat until gelatin is completely dissolved.
2. Remove from heat; add remaining 1½ cups water and the next 7 ingredients. Beat with rotary beater until well mixed. Chill until mixture is the consistency of thick, unbeaten egg white, stirring occasionally.
3. Fold in the vegetables and olives. Turn into a 1½-quart fancy mold which has been rinsed with cold water. Chill until firm.
4. Unmold onto a chilled serving plate and garnish with crisp *salad greens*.

6 TO 8 SERVINGS

## DANDELION AND LETTUCE SALAD

| | |
|---|---|
| 1 head lettuce, rinsed, drained, and chilled | Salt and pepper |
| 1 pt. dandelion greens, rinsed, drained, and chilled | 3 tablespoons olive oil |
| 4 small onions | ¼ cup vinegar |
| ½ green pepper | 2 medium tomatoes, cut in quarters |
| ⅓ lb. Swiss cheese | 2 hard-cooked eggs, sliced |

1. Cut lettuce, dandelion greens, onions, green

pepper, and cheese into small pieces. Sprinkle with salt and pepper to taste; toss lightly.
2. Drizzle with olive oil and vinegar; continue tossing and gently mix in tomatoes and eggs.

8 SERVINGS

## CRUMB CAKE

| | |
|---|---|
| 3 cups sifted all-purpose flour | 1 teaspoon ground nutmeg |
| 2 cups sugar | ⅛ teaspoon ground cloves |
| 1 cup butter or margarine | 1 cup pecans, coarsely chopped |
| 1 teaspoon baking soda | 1 cup dark seedless raisins |
| ½ teaspoon baking powder | 2 cups buttermilk |
| ⅛ teaspoon salt | |
| 4 teaspoons cocoa | |
| 2 tablespoons ground cinnamon | |

1. Sift flour and sugar together. Cut in butter with a pastry blender or two knives until pieces are size of small peas. Measure 1 cup of the crumb mixture and set aside for topping.
2. Add a mixture of baking soda, baking powder, salt, cocoa, spices, pecans, and raisins to the remaining crumb mixture; blend thoroughly. Add buttermilk and stir until just blended. Turn batter into a prepared 13x9x2-inch baking pan and spread evenly to edges. Sprinkle top with reserved crumb mixture.
3. Bake at 350°F about 1 hour, or until cake tests done.
4. Cool in pan on wire rack. Cut into squares.

ONE 13x9-INCH CAKE

## GINGERBREAD WITH CORIANDER

| | |
|---|---|
| 2¼ cups flour | ½ teaspoon ground nutmeg |
| 1 teaspoon baking soda | 1 teaspoon ground coriander |
| ½ teaspoon baking powder | 1 cup light molasses |
| ½ teaspoon salt | 1 cup boiling water |
| 2 tablespoons cocoa | ½ cup butter or margarine |
| 1 teaspoon ground cinnamon | ½ cup sugar |
| 1 teaspoon ground ginger | 1 egg |

1. Blend the first 9 ingredients thoroughly.
2. Combine molasses and water; set aside.
3. Beat butter until softened. Add sugar gradually,

creaming until fluffy. Add egg and beat thoroughly.
4. Alternately add dry ingredients in fourths and liquid in thirds to creamed mixture, beating until blended after each addition. Turn batter into a greased and waxed-paper-lined 9x9x2-inch pan; spread batter evenly.
5. Bake at 350°F 40 to 45 minutes, or until cake tests done. Cool slightly, then remove from pan.
6. Cut into squares while still warm and top with *sweetened whipped cream.*　　**ABOUT 9 SERVINGS**

## GINGERSNAP CUTOUTS

| | |
|---|---|
| ½ cup sugar | ¾ teaspoon baking soda |
| 1 cup shortening | ¼ teaspoon salt |
| 1 cup molasses | 2 teaspoons ground |
| 3½ cups sifted | ginger |
| all-purpose flour | |

1. Add the sugar gradually to the shortening, creaming until fluffy. Add the molasses gradually, beating thoroughly.
2. Sift flour, baking soda, salt, and ginger together; add in fourths to creamed mixture, mixing well after each addition.
3. Chill dough until firm enough to roll.
4. Working with a small amount of dough at a time, roll about 1/16 inch thick on a floured surface. Cut with a round 2½-inch cookie cutter. Place rounds on ungreased cookie sheets.
5. Bake at 375°F about 8 minutes.
6. Allow cookies to remain about 30 seconds on cookie sheets before removing to wire racks. Cool thoroughly.　　**ABOUT 6 DOZEN COOKIES**

## TERRA NOVA MOLASSES PIE

| | |
|---|---|
| Pastry for an 8-inch | 1 cup molasses |
| lattice-top pie | 1 cup soft bread |
| 1 egg | crumbs |

1. Prepare pastry shell and lattice strips.
2. Beat egg; add molasses and beat until mixed. Stir in bread crumbs. Pour into pastry shell. Top with lattice strips.
3. Bake at 400°F about 20 minutes, or until pastry is lightly browned and filling is firm.

**ONE 8-INCH PIE**

## LIME SNOW

| | |
|---|---|
| 1 pkg. lime-flavored | 2 tablespoons lemon |
| gelatin | juice |
| ¾ cup boiling water | 3 egg whites |
| 1 cup unsweetened | ¼ cup sugar |
| pineapple juice | |

1. Dissolve gelatin in boiling water in a bowl. Stir in the juices. Chill until mixture is slightly thickened, stirring occasionally.
2. Beat egg whites until frothy; gradually add sugar, beating constantly until stiff peaks are formed. Fold into thickened gelatin mixture.
3. Pile mixture into 6 sherbet glasses and chill until firm.　　**6 SERVINGS**

## MOLASSES BUTTER BRITTLE

| | |
|---|---|
| 1 cup sugar | 2 tablespoons water |
| ½ cup butter or | ½ teaspoon vanilla |
| margarine | extract |
| ¼ cup light molasses | |

1. Combine the sugar, butter, molasses, and water in a heavy 2-quart saucepan. Mix well and set over low heat; stir until sugar is dissolved. Increase heat and bring mixture to boiling. Wash crystals from sides of pan. Set candy thermometer in place.
2. Cook, stirring constantly, to 300°F (hard-crack stage).
3. Remove from heat and remove thermometer. Stir in vanilla extract. Pour syrup into a buttered 8-inch square pan; do not scrape saucepan.
4. Before candy cools, mark quickly into squares with a sharp knife; set aside to cool.
5. When hard, break candy into pieces. Store in tightly covered container in a cool dry place.

**ABOUT ¾ POUND CANDY**

## BAKEAPPLE JAM

Bakeapples or cloud berries are yellow in color, shaped like blackberries, and have a delicious flavor. Wash and weigh *berries.* Add ¾ *pound of sugar* to each 1 pound of berries. Combine and let stand overnight. In the morning, bring to a boil and simmer for 20 to 25 minutes. Pour into sterilized jars and seal.

**BAKEAPPLE PIE:** Fill a *baked pie crust* with *bakeapple jam* and serve with *clotted cream.*

# *Index*